No Greater Love

No Greater Love

MOTHER TERESA

Edited by
Becky Benenate & Joseph Durepos

New World Library
Novato, California

New World Library
14 Pamaron Way
Novato, California 94949

Cover design: Big Fish
Cover photo: © 1989 Raghu Rai / Magnum Photos, Inc.
Text design: Aaron Kenedi

Library of Congress Cataloging-in-Publication Data

Teresa, Mother, 1910 —
No greater love / Mother Teresa :
edited by Becky Benenate & Joseph Durepos
p. cm. Includes bibliographical references
ISBN 1-57731-006-3 (hardcover : alk. paper)
1. Christian life — Catholic authors. 2. Spiritual life — Catholic
Church. 3. Catholic Church — Doctrines. 4. Missionaries of Charity.
5. Teresa, Mother, 1910 — .
I. Benenate, Becky. II. Durepos, Joseph. III. Title

BX2350.2.T468 1997   96-43158
248.4'82—dc20   CIP

First printing, January 1997
Printed in U.S.A. on acid-free paper
ISBN 1-57731-006-3
Distributed to the trade by Publishers Group West
10 9 8 7 6 5 4 3 2 1

From the moment a soul has the grace to know God,
she must seek.

— MOTHER TERESA

TABLE OF CONTENTS

No Greater Love was originally published as *The Mother Teresa Reader, A Life for God,* compiled by LaVonne Neff. This new, completely revised and updated edition edited by Becky Benenate and Joseph Durepos.

◦⁀◦

Scripture texts used in this work, unless otherwise indicated, are taken from *The New American Bible (NAB)*. Selected texts are taken from *The Revised Standard Version of the Bible (RSV)*. Some scripture quotations are taken from the *Holy Bible: King James Version (KJV)*, or are Mother Teresa's own paraphrases.

FOREWORD

Mother Teresa has caught the imagination of the world not because she is a great writer or theologian, but because she is a person of immense compassion and openness. On one level she has been receptive to her calling, led first by inner promptings to enter a convent, then to focus her life work clearly and exclusively on service to the poor, and then to create her own religious community. Because of her undefended state, she feels the suffering of the world, of the old and the very young and those between. She knows firsthand the meaning of empathy and more so the profundity of pathos.

In the intimate reflections published in this

book, we learn some of the secrets of this person, often publicly recognized as small in physical stature but great in spirit, who stops to care precisely for those whom the world in general neglects. Her particular kind of Christianity, with its spiritual vision, methods of prayer, and inspiring figure of Jesus, she tells us, keeps her personal spirits and her unlimited compassion high.

To a sophisticated modern reader, some of her ideas and language, especially her piety, may seem naive and unnecessarily self-denying. As I read her thoughts, I'm led back in memory to my own early school days when I was taught by nuns to "mortify the body and the senses." But there is indeed wisdom in finding ways to silence the busy life and to become less preoccupied with self. For Mother Teresa, apparently her lifelong habit of quieting her ego through prayer has led to a vibrant life in the world and the rich development of her personality. Modern psychology has yet to discover what the religions have taught for millennia — that loss of self leads to the discovery of soul.

As I read her words, I try to hear them not as naive, but as sophisticated in a way that is largely foreign to modern taste. Rather than avoiding suffering, she becomes intimate with it. Rather than heroically trying to overcome death, in the style of modern Western medical philosophy, she focuses her attention on a person's emotional state and sense of meaning in the last moments. She is acutely attentive, too, to the feelings of children, a strong sign, in my estimation, of a person profoundly initiated in the ways of the soul.

In current psychological jargon, insight, self-awareness, and working on one's life are central in the project of becoming a self. But Mother Teresa could teach psychologists a thing or two, as when she tells the story of a woman who underwent profound personal change when, on Mother Teresa's astute advice, she began to wear less expensive dress. Beneath Mother Teresa's straightforward faith and personal honesty lies a subtle knowledge of human motivation.

Some readers might find Mother Teresa's Christian faith, so unapologetically presented in the language of love and prayer, an obstacle. Anxious, defensive, and proselytizing religion swirls around us daily, to the point that many find an institutional religion repugnant. To those readers I would suggest that they let go of certain literalistic and infantile meanings that they may attach to theological language, and hear the challenging message that Mother Teresa evidently senses in her faith. I can read a Buddhist exhorting me to see the Buddha-nature in an animal in much the same way I can be encouraged by Mother Teresa to see Jesus in a dying man or the mystical body of Christ in the community of humankind.

Too often religion is imagined and lived as a purely spiritual activity, sometimes as a mental exercise in belief and explanation. In Mother Teresa's life and words we find religion's soul, in the sense that her faith is inseparable from her compassion, and her compassion is never disconnected from her behavior. In a purely spiritual religion, a follower may profess beliefs loudly and intolerantly — I don't see much service to the poor and sick among those who would like us all to adopt their beliefs. When religion is largely mental, spiritual attitudes may never get translated into compassionate action in the world community.

What is absent in these passionate words of

Mother Teresa is any attempt to convert us to her beliefs. She simply describes her strong faith and tells us about her work with the poor and the sick. Her stories are obviously not meant to convince us of her religious convictions; rather, they simply demonstrate how human beings, when given the most basic kinds of love and attention, find significant transformation and discover their humanity, dignity, and at least momentary happiness.

Many describe Mother Teresa as a rare "living saint." I appreciate that sentiment. We need saints, just as we need some of the old words such as sin, grace, faith, and evil. Once, we could reflect on our experience philosophically and theologically; today we have reduced all analysis of our situation to the psychological, the sociological, and the political. These reductive ways of thinking render experience more narrow and superficial, while they give the illusion that if we could only become thoroughly hygienic we'd be free of our problems.

Mother Teresa doesn't speak or work within such a limited social scientific framework. Prayer and dedication are still relevant to her, and in them she finds her values and her life work. Thinking of her as a saint, we might consider her example impossible for us to emulate, but the reflections she captures in this book could show us, as she says, that we can all be saints — not without our imperfections and follies, not without our need to confess to failings daily, but nevertheless dedicated to the community of people, especially those in distress, who make up our family, our neighborhood, and our world.

— THOMAS MOORE
author of *Care of the Soul* and
Re-Enchantment of Everyday Life

No Greater Love

On Prayer

Prayer is in all things, in all gestures.

— MOTHER TERESA

Why are you sleeping?
Wake up, and pray . . .

— JESUS TO THE DISCIPLES

ASLEEP IN THE GARDEN, LUKE 22:46 NAB

I don't think there is anyone who needs God's help and grace as much as I do. Sometimes I feel so helpless and weak. I think that is why God uses me. Because I cannot depend on my own strength, I rely on Him twenty-four hours a day. If the day had even more hours, then I would need His help and grace during those hours as well. All of us must cling to God through prayer.

My secret is very simple: I pray. Through prayer I become one in love with Christ. I realize that praying to Him is loving Him.

In reality, there is only one true prayer, only one

substantial prayer: Christ Himself. There is only one voice that rises above the face of the earth: the voice of Christ. Perfect prayer does not consist in many words, but in the fervor of the desire which raises the heart to Jesus.

Love to pray. Feel the need to pray often during the day. Prayer enlarges the heart until it is capable of containing God's gift of Himself. Ask and seek and your heart will grow big enough to receive Him and keep Him as your own.

We want so much to pray properly and then we fail. We get discouraged and give up. If you want to pray better, you must pray more. God allows the failure but He does not want the discouragement. He wants us to be more childlike, more humble, more grateful in prayer, to remember we all belong to the mystical body of Christ, which is praying always.

We need to help each other in our prayers. Let us free our minds. Let's not pray long, drawn-out prayers, but let's pray short ones full of love. Let us pray on behalf of those who do not pray. Let us remember, if we want to be able to love, we must be able to pray!

Prayer that comes from the mind and heart is called mental prayer. We must never forget that we are bound toward perfection and should aim ceaselessly at it. The practice of daily mental prayer is necessary to reach that goal. Because it is the breath of life to our soul, holiness is impossible without it.

It is only by mental prayer and spiritual reading that we can cultivate the gift of prayer. Mental prayer is greatly fostered by simplicity — that is, forgetfulness of self by transcending of the body and of our senses, and by frequent aspirations that feed our prayer. "In mental prayer," says Saint John Vianney, "shut your eyes, shut your mouth, and open your heart." In vocal prayer we speak to God; in mental prayer he speaks to us. It is then that God pours Himself into us.

Our prayers should be burning words coming forth from the furnace of hearts filled with love. In your prayers, speak to God with great reverence and confidence. Do not drag behind or run ahead; do not shout or keep silent, but devoutly, with great sweetness, with natural simplicity, without any affectation, offer your praise to God with the whole of your heart and soul.

Just once, let the love of God take entire and absolute possession of your heart; let it become to your heart like a second nature; let your heart suffer nothing contrary to enter; let it apply itself continually to increase this love of God by seeking to please Him in all things and refusing Him nothing; let it accept as from His hand everything that happens to it; let it have a firm determination never to commit any fault deliberately and knowingly or, if it should fail, to be humbled and to rise up again at once — and such a heart will pray continually.

People are hungry for the Word of God that will give peace, that will give unity, that will give joy. But you cannot give what you don't have. That's why it is necessary to deepen your life of prayer.

Be sincere in your prayers. Sincerity is humility, and you acquire humility only by accepting humiliations. All that has been said about humility is not enough to teach you humility. All that you have read about humility is not enough to teach you humility. You learn humility only by accepting humiliations. And you will meet humiliation all through your life. The greatest humiliation is to know that you are nothing. This you come to know when you face God in prayer.

Often a deep and fervent look at Christ is the best prayer: I look at Him and He looks at me. When you come face to face with God, you cannot but know that you are nothing, that you have nothing.

It is difficult to pray if you don't know how to pray, but we must help ourselves to pray. The first means to use is silence. We cannot put ourselves directly in the presence of God if we do not practice internal and external silence.

The interior silence is very difficult, but we must make the effort. In silence we will find new energy and true unity. The energy of God will be ours to do all things well, and so will the unity of our thoughts with His thoughts, the unity of our prayers with His prayers, the unity of our actions with His actions, of our life with His life. Unity is the fruit of prayer, of humility, of love.

In the silence of the heart God speaks. If you face God in prayer and silence, God will speak to you. Then you will know that you are nothing. It is only when you realize your nothingness, your emptiness, that God can fill you with Himself. Souls of prayer are souls of great silence.

Silence gives us a new outlook on everything. We need silence to be able to touch souls. The essential thing is not what we say but what God says to us and through us. In that silence, He will listen to us; there He will speak to our soul, and there we will hear His voice.

Listen in silence, because if your heart is full of other things you cannot hear the voice of God. But when you have listened to the voice of God in the stillness of your heart, then your heart is filled with God. This will need much sacrifice, but if we really mean to pray and want to pray we must be ready to do it now. These are only the first steps toward prayer but if we never make the first step with a determination, we will not reach the last one: the presence of God.

This is what we have to learn right from the beginning: to listen to the voice of God in our heart, and then in the silence of the heart God speaks. Then from the fullness of our hearts, our mouth will have to speak. That is the connection. In the silence of the heart, God speaks and you have to listen. Then in the fullness of your heart, because it is full of God, full of love, full of compassion, full of faith, your mouth will speak.

Remember, before you speak, it is necessary to listen, and only then, from the fullness of your heart you speak and God listens.

The contemplatives and ascetics of all ages and religions have sought God in the silence and solitude of the desert, forest, and mountain. Jesus Himself spent forty days in the desert and the mountains, communing for long hours with the Father in the silence of the night.

We too are called to withdraw at certain intervals into deeper silence and aloneness with God, together as a community as well as personally. To be alone with Him, not with our books, thoughts, and memories but completely stripped of everything, to dwell lovingly in His presence — silent, empty, expectant, and motionless.

We cannot find God in noise or agitation. Nature: trees, flowers, and grass grow in silence. The stars, the moon, and the sun move in silence. What is essential is not what we say but what God tells us and what He tells others through us. In silence He listens to us; in silence He speaks to our souls. In silence we are granted the privilege of listening to His voice.

Silence of our eyes.
Silence of our ears.
Silence of our mouths.
Silence of our minds.
. . . in the silence of the heart
God will speak.

Silence of the heart is necessary so you can hear God everywhere — in the closing of the door, in the person who needs you, in the birds that sing, in the flowers, in the animals.

If we are careful of silence it will be easy to pray. There is so much talk, so much repetition, so much carrying on of tales in words and in writing. Our prayer life suffers so much because our hearts are not silent.

I shall keep the silence of my heart with greater care, so that in the silence of my heart I hear His words of comfort and from the fullness of my heart I comfort Jesus in the distressing disguise of the poor.

Real prayer is union with God, a union as vital as that of the vine to the branch, which is the illustration Jesus gives us in the Gospel of John. We need prayer. We need that union to produce good fruit. The fruit is what we produce with our hands, whether it be food, clothing, money, or something else. All of this is the fruit of our oneness with God. We need a life of prayer, of poverty, and of sacrifice to do it with love.

Sacrifice and prayer complement each other. There is no prayer without sacrifice, and there is no sacrifice without prayer. Jesus' life was spent in intimate union with His Father as He passed through this world. We need to do the same. Let's walk by His side. We need to give Christ a chance to make use of us, to be His word and His work, to share His food and His clothing in the world today.

If we do not radiate the light of Christ around us, the sense of the darkness that prevails in the world will increase.

We are called to love the world. And God loved the world so much that He gave Jesus. Today He loves the world so much that He gives you and me to be His love, His compassion, and His presence, through a life of prayer, of sacrifice, of surrender to God. The response that God asks of you is to be a contemplative.

If we take Jesus at His word, all of us are contemplatives in the heart of the world, for if we have faith, we are continually in His presence. By contemplation the soul draws directly from the heart of God the graces, which the active life must distribute. Our lives must be connected with the living Christ in us. If we do not live in the presence of God we cannot go on.

What is contemplation? To live the life of Jesus. This is what I understand. To love Jesus, to live His life in us, to live our life in His life. That's contemplation. We must have a clean heart to be able to see — no jealousy, anger, contention, and especially no uncharitableness. To me, contemplation is not to be locked in a dark place, but to allow Jesus to live His passion, His love, His humility in us, praying with us, being with us, and sanctifying through us.

Our contemplation is our life. It is not a matter of doing but being. It is the possession of our spirit by the Holy Spirit breathing into us the plenitude of God and sending us forth to the whole creation as His personal message of love.

We shall not waste our time in looking for extraordinary experiences in our life of contemplation but live by pure faith, ever watchful and ready for His coming by doing our day-to-day duties with extraordinary love and devotion.

Our life of contemplation simply put is to realize God's constant presence and His tender love for us in the least little things of life. To be constantly available to Him, loving Him with our whole heart, whole mind, whole soul, and whole strength, no matter in what form He may come to us. Does your mind and your heart go to Jesus as soon as you get up in the morning? This is prayer, that you turn your mind and heart to God.

Prayer is the very life of oneness, of being one with Christ. Therefore, prayer is as necessary as the air, as the blood in our body, as anything, to keep us alive to the grace of God. To pray generously is not enough; we must pray devoutly, with fervor and piety. We must pray perseveringly and with great love. If we don't pray, our presence will have no power, our words will have no power.

We need prayers in order to better carry out the work of God, and so that in every moment we may know how to be completely available to Him.

We should make every effort to walk in the presence of God, to see God in all the persons we meet, to live our prayer throughout the day.

Knowledge of the self puts us on our knees, and it is very necessary for love. For knowledge of God produces love, and knowledge of the self produces humility. Knowledge of the self is a very important thing in our lives. As Saint Augustine says, "Fill yourselves first, and then only will you be able to give to others."

Knowledge of the self is also a safeguard against pride, especially when you are tempted in life. The greatest mistake is to think you are too strong to fall into temptation. Put your finger in the fire and it will burn. So we have to go through the fire. The temptations are allowed by God. The only thing we have to do is to refuse to give in.

Prayer, to be fruitful, must come from the heart and must be able to touch the heart of God. See how Jesus taught His disciples to pray. I believe each time we say "Our Father," God looks at His hands, where He has carved us. ("I have carved you on the palm of my hand." See Isaiah 49:16.) He looks at His hands, and He sees us there. How wonderful the tenderness and love of God!

If we pray the "Our Father," and live it, we will be holy. Everything is there: God, myself, my neighbor. If I forgive, then I can be holy and can pray. All this comes from a humble heart, and if we have this we will know how to love God, to love self, and to love our neighbor. This is not complicated, and yet we complicate our lives so much, by so many additions. Just one thing counts — to be humble, to pray. The more you pray, the better you will pray.

A child has no difficulty expressing his little mind in simple words that say so much. Jesus said to Nicodemus: "Become as a little child." If we pray the gospel, we will allow Christ to grow in us. So pray lovingly like children, with an earnest desire to love much and to make loved the one that is not loved.

All our words will be useless unless they come from within. Words that do not give the light of Christ increase the darkness. Today, more than ever, we need to pray for the light to know the will of God, for the love to accept the will of God, for the way to do the will of God.

For me, prayer means launching out of the heart toward God; a cry of grateful love from the crest of joy or the trough of despair; it is a vast, supernatural force that opens out my heart, and binds me close to Jesus.

— SAINT THERESE OF LISIEUX

I give you my word, if you are ready to believe that you will receive whatever you ask for in prayer, it shall be done for you.

— JESUS, MARK 11:24 NAB

On Love

Love each other as God loves each one of you, with an intense and particular love.

Be kind to each other: It is better to commit faults with gentleness than to work miracles with unkindness.

— MOTHER TERESA

By this evidence everyone will know that you are my disciples — if you have love for one another.

— JESUS, JOHN 13:35 RSV

Jesus came into this world for one purpose. He came to give us the good news that God loves us, that God is love, that He loves you, and He loves me. How did Jesus love you and me? By giving His life.

God loves us with a tender love. That is all that Jesus came to teach us: the tender love of God. "I have called you by your name, you are mine" (Isaiah 43:1 NAB).

The whole gospel is very, very simple. Do you love me? Obey my commandments. He's turning and twisting just to get around to one thing: love one another.

"Thou shalt love the Lord thy God with thy

whole heart, with thy whole soul, and with all thy mind" (Deuteronomy 6:5 KJV). This is the command of our great God, and He cannot command the impossible. Love is a fruit, in season at all times and within the reach of every hand. Anyone may gather it and no limit is set.

Everyone can reach this love through meditation, the spirit of prayer, and sacrifice, by an intense interior life. Do not think that love, in order to be genuine, has to be extraordinary.

What we need is to love without getting tired. How does a lamp burn? Through the continuous input of small drops of oil. What are these drops of oil in our lamps? They are the small things of daily life: faithfulness, small words of kindness, a thought for others, our way of being silent, of looking, of speaking, and of acting. Do not look for Jesus away from yourselves. He is not out there; He is in you. Keep your lamp burning, and you will recognize Him.

These words of Jesus, "Even as I have loved you that you also love one another," should be not only a light to us, but they should also be a flame consuming the selfishness that prevents the growth of holiness. Jesus "loved us to the end," to the very limit of love: the cross. This love must come from within, from our union with Christ. Loving must be as normal to us as living and breathing, day after day until our death.

I have experienced many human weaknesses, many human frailties, and I still experience them. But we need to use them. We need to work for Christ with a humble heart, with the humility of Christ. He comes and uses us to be His love and compassion in the world in spite of our weaknesses and frailties.

One day I picked up a man from the gutter. His body was covered with worms. I brought him to our house, and what did this man say? He did not curse. He did not blame anyone. He just said, "I've lived like an animal in the street, but I'm going to die like an angel, loved and cared for!" It took us three hours to clean him. Finally, the man looked up at the sister and said, "Sister, I'm going home to God."

And then he died. I've never seen such a radiant smile on a human face as the one I saw on that man's face. He went home to God. See what love can do! It is possible that young sister did not think about it at the moment, but she was touching the body of Christ. Jesus said so when He said, "As often as you did it for one of my least brothers, you did it for me" (Matthew 25:40 RSV). And this is where you and I fit into God's plan.

Let us understand the tenderness of God's love. For He speaks in the Scripture, "Even if a mother could forget her child, I will not forget you. I have carved you on the palm of my hand" (see Isaiah 49:15-16). When you feel lonely, when you feel unwanted, when you feel sick and forgotten, remember you are precious to Him. He loves you. Show that love for one another, for this is all that Jesus came to teach us.

I remember a mother of twelve children, the last of them terribly mutilated. It is impossible for me to describe that creature. I volunteered to welcome the child into our house, where there are many others in similar conditions. The woman began to cry. "For God's sake, Mother," she said, "don't tell me that. This creature is the greatest gift of God to me and my family. All our love is focused on her. Our lives would be empty if you took her from us." Hers was a love full of understanding and tenderness. Do we have a love like that today? Do we realize that our child, our husband, our wife, our father, our mother, our sister or brother, has a need for that understanding, for the warmth of our hand?

I will never forget one day in Venezuela when I went to visit a family who had given us a lamb. I went to thank them and there I found out that they had a badly crippled child. I asked the mother, "What is the child's name?" The mother gave me a most beautiful answer. "We call him 'Teacher of Love,' because he keeps on teaching us how to love. Everything we do for him is our love for God in action."

We have a great deal of worth in the eyes of God. I never tire of saying over and over again that God loves us. It is a wonderful thing that God Himself loves me tenderly. That is why we should have courage, joy, and the conviction that nothing can separate us from the love of Christ.

∽

I feel that we too often focus only on the negative aspect of life — on what is bad. If we were more willing to see the good and the beautiful things that surround us, we would be able to transform our families. From there, we would change our next-door neighbors and then others who live in our neighborhood or city. We would be able to bring peace and love to our world, which hungers so much for these things.

If we really want to conquer the world, we will not be able to do it with bombs or with other weapons of destruction. Let us conquer the world with our love. Let us interweave our lives with bonds of sacrifice and love, and it will be possible for us to conquer the world.

We do not need to carry out grand things in order to show a great love for God and for our neighbor. It is the intensity of love we put into our gestures that makes them into something beautiful for God.

Peace and war start within one's own home. If we really want peace for the world, let us start by loving one another within our families. Sometimes it is hard for us to smile at one another. It is often difficult for the husband to smile at his wife or for the wife to smile at her husband.

In order for love to be genuine, it has to be above all a love for our neighbor. We must love those who are nearest to us, in our own family. From there, love spreads toward whoever may need us.

It is easy to love those who live far away. It is not always easy to love those who live right next to us. It is easier to offer a dish of rice to meet the hunger of a needy person than to comfort the loneliness and the anguish of someone in our own home who does not feel loved.

I want you to go and find the poor in your homes. Above all, your love has to start there. I want you to be the good news to those around you. I want you to be concerned about your next-door neighbor. Do you know who your neighbor is?

True love is love that causes us pain, that hurts, and yet brings us joy. That is why we must pray to God and ask Him to give us the courage to love.

From the abundance of the heart the mouth speaks. If your heart is full of love, you will speak of love. I want you all to fill your hearts with great love. Don't imagine that love, to be true and burning, must be extraordinary. No; what we need in our love is the continuous desire to love the One we love.

One day I found among the debris a woman who was burning with fever. About to die, she kept repeating, "It is my son who has done it!" I took her in my arms and carried her home to the convent. On the way I urged her to forgive her son. It took a good while before I could hear her say, "Yes, I forgive him." She said it with a feeling of genuine forgiveness, just as she was about to pass away. The woman was not aware that she was suffering, that she was burning with fever, that she was dying. What was breaking her heart was her own son's lack of love.

Holy souls sometimes undergo great inward trial, and they know darkness. But if we want others to become aware of the presence of Jesus, we must be the first ones convinced of it.

There are thousands of people who would love to have what we have, yet God has chosen us to be where we are today to share the joy of loving others. He wants us to love one another, to give ourselves to each other until it hurts. It does not matter how much we give, but how much love we put into our giving.

In the words of our Holy Father, each one of us must be able "to cleanse what is dirty, to warm what is lukewarm, to strengthen what is weak, to enlighten what is dark." We must not be afraid to proclaim Christ's love and to love as He loved.

Where God is, there is love; and where there is love, there always is an openness to serve. The world is hungry for God.

When we all see God in each other, we will love one another as He loves us all. That is the fulfillment of the law, to love one another. This is all Jesus came to teach us: that God loves us, and that He wants us to love one another as He loves us.

We must know that we have been created for

greater things, not just to be a number in the world, not just to go for diplomas and degrees, this work and that work. We have been created in order to love and to be loved.

∽

Always be faithful in little things, for in them our strength lies. To God nothing is little. He cannot make anything small; they are infinite. Practice fidelity in the least things, not for their own sake, but for the sake of the great thing that is the will of God, and which I respect greatly.

Do not pursue spectacular deeds. We must deliberately renounce all desires to see the fruit of our labor, doing all we can as best we can, leaving the rest in the hands of God. What matters is the gift of your self, the degree of love that you put into each one of your actions.

Do not allow yourselves to be disheartened by any failure as long as you have done your best. Neither glory in your success, but refer all to God in deepest thankfulness.

If you are discouraged, it is a sign of pride

because it shows you trust in your own powers. Never bother about people's opinions. Be humble and you will never be disturbed. The Lord has willed me here where I am. He will offer a solution.

When we handle the sick and the needy we touch the suffering body of Christ and this touch will make us heroic; it will make us forget the repugnance and the natural tendencies in us. We need the eyes of deep faith to see Christ in the broken body and dirty clothes under which the most beautiful one among the sons of men hides. We shall need the hands of Christ to touch these bodies wounded by pain and suffering. Intense love does not measure — it just gives.

Our works of charity are nothing but the overflow of our love of God from within.

Charity is like a living flame: The drier the fuel, the livelier the flame. Likewise, our hearts, when they are free of all earthly causes, commit themselves in free service. Love of God must give rise to a total service. The more disgusting the work, the greater must love be, as it takes succor to the Lord disguised in the rags of the poor.

Charity, to be fruitful, must cost us. Actually, we hear so much about charity, yet we never give it its full importance: God put the commandment of loving our neighbor on the same footing as the first commandment.

In order for us to be able to love, we need to have faith because faith is love in action; and love in action is service. In order for us to be able to love, we have to see and touch. Faith in action through prayer, faith in action through service: each is the same thing, the same love, the same compassion.

Some years have gone by, but I will never forget a young French girl who came to Calcutta. She looked so worried. She went to work in our home for dying destitutes. Then, after ten days, she came to see me. She hugged me and said, "I've found Jesus!" I asked where she found Jesus. "In the home for dying destitutes," she answered. "And what did you do after you found Him?" "I went to confession and Holy Communion for the first time in fifteen years." Then I said again, "What else did you do?" "I sent my parents a telegram saying that I found Jesus." I looked at her and I said, "Now, pack up and go home. Go home and give joy, love, and peace to your parents." She went home radiating joy, because her heart was filled with joy; and what joy she brought to her family! Why? Because she had lost the innocence of her youth and had gotten it back again.

God loves a cheerful giver. The best way to show your gratitude to God and people is to accept everything with joy. A joyful heart is a normal result of a heart burning with love. Joy is strength. The poor felt attracted to Jesus because a higher power dwelt in Him and flowed from Him — out of His eyes, His hands, His body — completely released and present to God and to men.

Let nothing so disturb us, so fill us with sorrow or discouragement, as to make us forfeit the joy of the resurrection. Joy is not simply a matter of temperament in the service of God and souls; it is always hard. All the more reason why we should try to acquire it and make it grow in our hearts. We may not be able to give much but we can always give the joy that springs from a heart that is in love with God.

All over the world people are hungry and thirsty for God's love. We meet that hunger by spreading joy. Joy is one of the best safeguards against temptation. Jesus can take full possession of our soul only if it surrenders itself joyfully.

Someone once asked me, "Are you married?" And I said, "Yes, and I find it sometimes very difficult to smile at Jesus because He can be very demanding."

God is within me with a more intimate presence than that whereby I am in myself: "In Him we live and move and have our being" (Acts 17:28 NAB). It is He who gives life to all, who gives power and being to all that exists. But for His sustaining presence, all things would cease to be and fall back into nothingness. Consider that you are in God, surrounded and encompassed by God, swimming in God. God's love is infinite. With God, nothing is impossible.

At the end of our life, we shall be judged by love.

— SAINT JOHN OF THE CROSS

For God so loved the world that He gave His only Son, so that everyone who believes in Him may not perish but may have eternal life.

— JESUS, JOHN 3:16 RSV

On Giving

Give of your hands to serve and your hearts to love.
— MOTHER TERESA

Truly I tell you, this poor widow has put in more than all those who are contributing to the treasury. For all of them have contributed out of their abundance; but she out of her poverty has put in everything she had. . . .
— JESUS, MARK 12:43-44 RSV

I will tell you a story. One night a man came to our house and told me, "There is a family with eight children. They have not eaten for days."

I took some food with me and went. When I came to that family, I saw the faces of those little children disfigured by hunger. There was no sorrow or sadness in their faces, just the deep pain of hunger. I gave the rice to the mother. She divided the rice in two, and went out, carrying half the rice. When she came back, I asked her, "Where did you go?" She gave me this simple answer, "To my neighbors; they are hungry also!" I was not surprised that she gave — poor people are really very generous. I was surprised that she knew they were hungry. As a rule, when we are suffering, we are so focused on ourselves, we have no time for others.

❦

Here in Calcutta we have a number of non-Christians and Christians who work together in the house of the dying and other places. There are also some who offer their care to the lepers. One day an Australian man came and made a substantial donation. But as he did this he said, "This is something external. Now I want to give something of myself." He now comes regularly to the house of the dying to shave the sick men and to converse with them. This man gives not only his money but also his time. He could have spent it on himself, but what he wants is to give himself.

I often ask for gifts that have nothing to do with money. There are always things one can get. What I desire is the presence of the donor, for him to touch those to whom he gives, for him to smile at them, to pay attention to them.

If our poor die of hunger, it is not because God does not care for them. Rather, it is because neither you nor I are generous enough. It is because we are not instruments of love in the hands of God. We do not recognize Christ when once again He appears to us in the hungry man, in the lonely woman, in the child who is looking for a place to get warm.

Sometimes the rich seem very willing to share in their own way, but it is a pity that they never give to the point of feeling that they are in need. The present generations, especially children, understand better. There are English children who make sacrifices in order to be able to offer a muffin to our children. There are Danish children who make sacrifices in order to be able to offer others a glass of milk every day. And German children do the same in order to be able to offer the poor some fortified food. These are concrete ways of teaching love. When these children grow up, they will know what it means to give.

Some time ago I made a trip to Ethiopia. Our sisters were working there during that terrible drought. Just as I was about to leave for Ethiopia, I found myself surrounded by many children. Each one of them gave something. "Take this to the children! Take this to the children!" they would say. They had many gifts that they wanted to give to our poor. Then a small child, who for the first time had a piece of chocolate, came up to me and said, "I do not want to eat it. You take it and give it to the children." This little one gave a great deal, because he gave it all, and he gave something that was very precious to him.

Have you ever experienced the joy of giving? I do not want you to give to me from your abundance. I never allow people to have fund-raisers for me. I don't want that. I want you to give of yourself. The love you put into the giving is the most important thing.

I don't want people donating just to get rid of something. There are people in Calcutta who have so much money that they want to get rid of it. They sometimes have money to spare, money that they try to hide.

A few days ago I received a package wrapped in plain paper. I thought that it might contain stamps, cards, or something like that, so I put it aside. I planned to open it later when I had the time. A few hours later I opened it without even suspecting its contents. It was hard for me to believe my eyes. That package contained twenty thousand rupees. It didn't have a return address or any note, which made me think that it might be money owed to the government.

I don't like people to send me something because they want to get rid of it. Giving is something different. It is sharing.

I also don't want you to give me what you have left over. I want you to give from *your want* until you really feel it!

The other day I received fifteen dollars from a man who has been paralyzed for twenty years. The paralysis only allows him the use of his right hand. The only company he tolerates is tobacco. He told me, "I have stopped smoking for a week. I'm sending you the money I've saved from not buying cigarettes." It must have been a horrible sacrifice for him. I bought bread with his money, and I gave it to those who were hungry. So both the giver and those who received experienced joy.

This is something all of us need to learn. The

chance to share our love with others is a gift from God. May it be for us just as it was for Jesus. Let's love one another as He has loved us. Let's love one another with undivided love. Let's experience the joy of loving God and loving one another.

There are many medicines and cures for all kinds of sicknesses. But unless kind hands are given in service and generous hearts are given in love, I do not think there can ever be a cure for the terrible sickness of feeling unloved.

None of us has the right to condemn anyone. Even when we see people doing bad and we don't know why they do it. Jesus invites us not to pass judgment. Maybe we are the ones who have helped make them what they are. We need to realize that they are our brothers and sisters. That leper, that drunkard, and that sick person are our brothers because they too have been created for a greater love. This is something that we should never forget. Jesus Christ identifies Himself with them and says, "Whatever you did to the least of my brethren, you did it to me." Perhaps it is because we haven't given them our understanding and love that they find themselves on the streets without love and care.

Be kind, very kind, to the suffering poor. We little realize what they go through. The most difficult part is not being wanted.

One thing will always secure heaven for us: the acts of charity and kindness with which we have filled our lives. We will never know how much good just a simple smile can do. We tell people how kind, forgiving, and understanding God is, but are we the living proof? Can they really see this kindness, this forgiveness, this understanding alive in us?

Let us be very sincere in our dealings with each other and have the courage to accept each other as we are. Do not be surprised or become preoccupied at each other's failure; rather see and find the good in each other, for each one of us is created in the image of God. Keep in mind that our community is not composed of those who are already saints, but of those who are trying to become saints. Therefore, let us be extremely patient with each other's faults and failures.

Use your tongue for the good of others, for out of the abundance of the heart the mouth speaks. We have to possess before we can give. Those who have the mission of giving to others must grow first in the knowledge of God.

Not so long ago a very wealthy Hindu lady came to see me. She sat down and told me, "I would like to share in your work." In India, more and more people like her are offering to help. I said, "That is fine." The poor woman had a weakness that she confessed to me. "I love elegant saris," she said. Indeed, she had on a very expensive sari that probably cost around eight hundred rupees. Mine cost only eight rupees. Hers cost one hundred times more.

Then I asked the Virgin Mary to help me give an adequate answer to her question of how she could share in our work. It occurred to me to say to her, "I would start with the saris. The next time you go to buy one, instead of paying eight hundred rupees, buy one that costs five hundred. Then with the extra three hundred rupees, buy saris for the poor." The good woman now wears 100-rupee saris, and that is because I have asked her not to buy cheaper ones. She has confessed to me that this has changed her life. She now knows what it means to share. That woman assures me that she has received more than what she has given.

I think that a person who is attached to riches, who lives with the worry of riches, is actually very poor. However, if such a person puts her money at the service of others, then she is rich, very rich.

Kindness has converted more people than zeal, science, or eloquence. Holiness grows so fast where there is kindness. The world is lost for want of sweetness and kindness. Do not forget we need each other.

There is a natural conscience in every human being to know right from wrong. I deal with thousands who are Christians and non-Christians, and you can see such a conscience at work in their lives, drawing them to God. In everybody there is a tremendous hunger for God. If everyone were capable of discovering the image of God in their neighbors, do you think that we would still need tanks and generals?

Love Him totally who gave Himself totally for your love.

— SAINT CLARE OF ASSISI

Give, and it shall be given unto you. . . .

— JESUS, LUKE 6:38 KJV

On Being Holy

∽

Our mission is to convey God's love — not a dead God but a living God, a God of love.

— MOTHER TERESA

Teach them to carry out everything I have commanded you. And know that I am with you always, until the end of the world!

— JESUS, MATTHEW 28:20 NAB

We should not be concerned with the instrument God uses to speak to us, but with what God is saying to us. I'm just a little pencil in His hand. Tomorrow, if He finds somebody more helpless, more hopeless, I think He will do still greater things with her and through her.

We all know that there is a God who loves us, who has made us. We can turn and ask Him, "My Father, help me now. I want to be holy, I want to be good, I want to love." Holiness is not a luxury for the few; it is not just for some people. It is meant for you and for me and for all of us. It is a simple duty, because if we learn to love, we learn to be holy.

The first step to becoming holy is to will it. Jesus wants us to be holy as His Father is. Holiness consists of carrying out God's will with joy.

The words "I want to be holy" mean: I will divest myself of everything that is not of God; I will divest myself and empty my heart of material things. I will renounce my own will, my inclinations, my whims, my fickleness; and I will become a generous slave to God's will.

With a will that is whole I will love God, I will opt for Him, I will run toward Him, I will reach Him, I will possess Him. But it all depends on these words: "I want" or "I do not want." I have to pour all of my energy into the words "I want."

To become holy we need humility and prayer. Jesus taught us how to pray, and He also told us to learn from Him to be meek and humble of heart. Neither of these can we do unless we know what silence is. Both humility and prayer grow from an ear, mind, and tongue that have lived in silence with God, for in the silence of the heart God speaks.

Let us really take the trouble to learn the lesson of holiness from Jesus, whose heart was meek and humble. The first lesson from this heart is an examination of our conscience, and the rest — love and service — follow at once.

Examination is not our work alone, but a partnership between us and Jesus. We should not waste our time in useless looks at our own miseries, but should lift our hearts to God and let His light enlighten us.

If you are humble, nothing will touch you, neither praise nor disgrace, because you know what you are. If you are blamed, you won't be discouraged; if anyone calls you a saint, you won't put yourself on a pedestal. If you are a saint, thank God; if you are a sinner, don't remain one. Christ tells us to aim very high, not to be like Abraham or David or any of the saints, but to be like our heavenly Father.

> *You did not choose me, but I chose you. . . .*
>
> — JESUS, JOHN 15:16 RSV

I have the impression that the passion of Christ is being relived everywhere. Are we willing to share in this passion? Are we willing to share people's sufferings, not only in poor countries but all over the world? It seems to me that this great poverty of suffering in the West is much harder to solve. When I pick up some starving person off the street and offer him a bowl of rice or a piece of bread, I can satisfy his hunger. But a person that has been beaten or feels unwanted or unloved or fearful or rejected by society experiences a kind of poverty that is much more painful and deep. The cure is much more difficult to find.

People are hungry for God. People are hungry for love. Are we aware of that? Do we know that? Do we see that? Do we have eyes to see? Quite often we look but we don't see. We are all just passing through this world. We need to open our eyes and see.

Since we cannot see Christ, we cannot express our love to Him. But we do see our neighbor, and we can do for him what we would do for Christ if He were visible. Let us be open to God, so that He can use us. Let us put love into action. Let us begin with our family, with our closest neighbors. It is difficult, but that is where our work begins. We are collaborators with Christ, fertile branches on the vine.

Remember, it is the individual that is important to us. In order to love a person, one must come close to him or her. If we wait until there is a given number of people, we will get lost in numbers and will never be able to show respect and love for one concrete person. To me, every person in the world is unique.

When our sisters were in Ceylon, a minister of state once told me something very surprising. He said, "You know, Mother, I love Christ but I hate Christians." So I asked him how that could be. He answered, "Because Christians do not give us Christ; they do not live their Christian lives to the fullest." Gandhi said something very similar: "If Christians were to live their Christian lives to the fullest, there would not be one Hindu left in India." Isn't it very true? This love of Christ should urge us to spend ourselves without ceasing.

The perfect will of God for us: You must be holy. Holiness is the greatest gift that God can give us because for that reason He created us.

Submission, for a person who loves, is more than a duty; it is the secret of holiness.

Saint Francis said each one of us is what he is in the eyes of God — nothing more, nothing less. We are all called to be saints. There is nothing extraordinary about this call. We all have been created in the image of God to love and to be loved.

Jesus desires our perfection with unspeakable ardor. "It is God's will that you grow in holiness" (1 Thessalonians 4:3 NAB). His Sacred Heart is filled with an insatiable longing to see us advance toward holiness.

We ought every day to renew our resolution and to rouse ourselves to fervor, as if it were the first day of our conversion, saying, "Help me, Lord God, in my good resolve and in thy holy service, and give me grace this very day really and truly to begin, for what I have done till now is nothing." We cannot be renewed without the humility to recognize what needs to be renewed in ourselves.

Don't be afraid. There must be the cross, there must be suffering, a clear sign that Jesus has drawn you so close to His heart that He can share His suffering with you. Without God we can spread only pain and suffering around us.

We all long for heaven where God is, but we have it in our power to be in heaven with Him right now, to be happy with Him at this very moment. But being happy with Him now means loving like He loves, helping like He helps, giving as He gives, serving as He serves, rescuing as He rescues, being with Him twenty-four hours a day, touching Him in His distressing disguise.

Jesus is going to do great things with you if you let Him, and if you don't try to interfere with Him. We interfere with God's plans when we push in someone or something else not suitable for us. Be strict with yourself, and then be very strict with what you are receiving from the outside. People may come with wonderful ideas, with beautiful things, but anything that takes you away from the reality of what you have given to God must remain outside.

Let us ask our Lord to be with us in our moments of temptation. We must not be afraid, because God loves us and will not fail to help us. Hence, have a deep reverence for our own person; reverence for others, treating all with accepted marks of courtesy, but abstaining from sentimental feelings or ill-ordered affections.

No need for us to despair. No need for us to be discouraged. No need, if we have understood the tenderness of God's love. You are precious to Him. He loves you, and He loves you so tenderly that He has carved you on the palm of His hand. When your heart feels restless, when your heart feels hurt, when your heart feels like breaking, remember, "I am precious to Him. He loves me. He has called me by my name. I am His. He loves me. God loves me." And to prove that love He died on the cross.

How unlike Him we are. How little love, how little compassion, how little forgiveness, how little kindness we have. We are not worthy to be so close to Him — to enter His heart. Let us find out what part of His body is wounded by our sins. Let us not go alone but put our hands in His. Our Father loves us. He has given us a name. We belong to Him with all our misery, our sin, our weakness, our goodness. We are His. Our way of life depends on our being rooted in Christ Jesus our Lord by our deliberate choice.

In India, I was asked by some government

people, "Don't you want to make us all Christians?" I said, "Naturally, I would like to give the treasure I have to you, but I cannot. I can only pray for you to receive it."

Once, someone asked me, "Why do you go abroad? Don't you have enough poor in India?" So I answered, "Jesus told us to go and preach to all the nations." That is why we go all over the world to preach His love and compassion.

Another time, an Indian physician, as he saw the care a sister devoted to a sick man who had been declared hopeless by his colleagues, said, "I came here without God. I'm now going back with God."

The work of moral rearmament is carried out with discretion and love. The more discrete, the more penetrating it will be. You give it to others, and it is they who absorb it.

We shall instruct by the power of the example of our lives lived entirely in and with Jesus Christ our Lord, bearing witness to the truth of the gospel by our single-minded devotion to and burning love of Christ and His Church, and also by verbal proclamation of the Word of God fearlessly, openly, and clearly, according to the teaching of the Church, whenever opportunity offers.

We shall sustain the tempted by our prayer, penance, and understanding love, and when opportunity offers, also by enlightening and encouraging words. We shall befriend the friendless and comfort the sick and sorrowful by our real love and personal concern for them, identifying ourselves with them in their pain and sorrow and by praying with them for God's healing and comfort and by encouraging them to offer their sufferings to the Lord for the salvation of the whole world.

We shall bear wrongs patiently by offering no resistance to the wicked. If anyone hits us on the right cheek we shall turn the left also; if anyone takes away anything from us, we shall not try to get it back. We shall forgive injuries by seeking no revenge but returning good for evil, by loving our enemies and praying for those who persecute us and blessing those who curse us.

The path of loving trust means:

. . . an absolute, unconditional, and unwavering confidence in God our loving Father, even when everything seems to be a total failure.

. . . to look to Him alone as our help and protector.

. . . to stop doubting and being discouraged, casting all our worries and cares on the Lord, and to walk in total freedom.

. . . to be daring and absolutely fearless of any obstacle, knowing that nothing is impossible with God.

. . . total reliance on our Heavenly Father with the spontaneous abandonment of little children, totally convinced of our utter nothingness but trusting to the point of rashness with courageous confidence in His fatherly goodness.

Let us thank God for all His love for us, in so many ways and in so many places. Let us in return, as an act of gratitude and adoration, determine to be holy because He is holy.

The moment I realized that God existed, I knew that I could not do otherwise than to live for Him alone. . . .

Faith strips the mask from the world and reveals God in everything. It makes nothing impossible and renders meaningless such words as anxiety, danger, and fear, so that the believer goes through life calmly and peacefully, with profound joy — like a child, hand in hand with his mother.

— CHARLES DE FOUCAULD

Do you now believe?

The hour is coming, indeed it has come, when you will be scattered, each one to his home. . . . Yet I am not alone because the Father is with me. I have said this to you, so that in me you may have peace. In the world you face persecution. But take courage; I have conquered the world!

— JESUS, JOHN 16:31-33 RSV

On Work & Service

I believe that if God finds a person more useless than me, He will do even greater things through her because this work is His.

— MOTHER TERESA

My grace is sufficient for you, for power is made perfect in weakness.

— JESUS TO PAUL,

II CORINTHIANS 12:9 RSV

It is possible that I may not be able to keep my attention fully on God while I work, but God doesn't demand that I do so. Yet I can fully desire and intend that my work be done with Jesus and for Jesus. This is beautiful and that is what God wants. He wants our will and our desire to be for Him, for our family, for our children, for our brethren, and for the poor.

Each one of us is merely a small instrument. When you look at the inner workings of electrical things, often you see small and big wires, new and old, cheap and expensive lined up. Until the current passes through them there will be no light. That wire is you and me. The current is God.

We have the power to let the current pass through us, use us, produce the light of the world. Or we can refuse to be used and allow darkness to spread.

It's possible that in the apartment or house across from yours there is a blind man who would be thrilled if you would go over and read the newspaper to him. It's possible that there is a family that needs something that seems insignificant to you, something as simple as having someone baby-sit their child for half an hour. There are so many little things that are so small many people almost forget about them.

If you are working in the kitchen do not think it does not require brains. Do not think that sitting, standing, coming, and going, that everything you do, is not important to God.

God will not ask how many books you have read; how many miracles you have worked; He will ask you if you have done your best, for the love of Him. Can you in all sincerity say, "I have done my best"? Even if the best is failure, it must be our best, our utmost.

If you are really in love with Christ, no matter how small your work, it will be done better; it will be wholehearted. Your work will prove your love.

You may be exhausted with work, you may even kill yourself, but unless your work is interwoven with love, it is useless. To work without love is slavery.

If someone feels that God wants from him a transformation of social structures, that's an issue between him and his God. We all have the duty to serve God where we feel called. I feel called to help individuals, to love each human being. I never think in terms of crowds in general but in terms of persons. Were I to think about crowds, I would never begin anything. It is the person that matters. I believe in person-to-person encounters.

The fullness of our heart comes in our actions: how I treat that leper, how I treat that dying person, how I treat the homeless. Sometimes it is more difficult to work with the street people than with the people in our homes for the dying because they are peaceful and waiting; they are ready to go to God.

You can touch the sick, the leper and believe that it is the body of Christ you are touching, but it is much more difficult when these people are drunk or shouting to think that this is Jesus in His distressing disguise. How clean and loving our hands must be to be able to bring that compassion to them!

We need to be pure in heart to see Jesus in the person of the spiritually poorest. Therefore, the more disfigured the image of God is in that person, the greater will be our faith and devotion in seeking Jesus' face and lovingly ministering to Him. We consider it an honor to serve Christ in the distressing disguise of the spiritually poorest; we do it with deep gratitude and reverence in a spirit of sharing.

The more repugnant the work, the greater the effect of love and cheerful service. If I had not first picked up the woman who was eaten by rats — her face, and legs, and so on — I could not have been a **Missionary of Charity**. **Feelings** of repugnance are human. If we give our wholehearted, free service in spite of such feelings, we will become holy. Saint Francis of Assisi was repulsed by lepers but he overcame it.

Whatever you do, even if you help somebody cross the road, you do it to Jesus. Even giving somebody a glass of water, you do it to Jesus. Such a simple little teaching, but it is more and more important.

We must not be afraid to proclaim Christ's love and to love as He loved. In the work we have to do it does not matter how small and humble it may be, make it Christ's love in action.

However beautiful the work is, be detached from it, even ready to give it up. The work is not yours. The talents God has given you are not yours; they have been given to you for your use, for the glory of God. Be great and use everything in you for the good Master.

What have we to learn? To be meek and humble; if we are meek and humble, we will learn to pray. If we learn to pray, we will belong to Jesus. If we belong to Jesus, we will learn to believe, and if we believe we will learn to love, and if we love we will learn to serve.

Spend your time in prayer. If you pray you will have faith, and if you have faith you will naturally want to serve. The one who prays cannot but have faith, and when you have faith you want to put it into action. Faith in action is service.

The fruit of love is service. Love leads us to say, "I want to serve." And the fruit of service is peace. All of us should work for peace.

Someone asked me what advice I had for politicians. I don't like to get involved in politics, but my answer just popped out, "They should spend time on their knees. I think that would help them to become better statesmen."

Strive to be the demonstration of God in the midst of your community. Sometimes we see how joy returns to the lives of the most destitute when they realize that many among us are concerned about them and show them our love. Even their health improves if they are sick.

May we never forget that in the service to the poor we are offered a magnificent opportunity to do something beautiful for God. In fact, when we give ourselves with all our hearts to the poor, it is Christ whom we are serving in their disfigured faces. For He Himself said, "You did it for me."

Daily Prayer of the Co-workers of Mother Teresa

Make us worthy, Lord, to serve our fellow men throughout the world who live and die in poverty and hunger.

Give them, through our hands, this day their daily bread, and by our understanding Love, give Peace and Joy.

Lord, make me a channel of Thy Peace, that where there is hatred, I may bring Love; that where there is wrong, I may bring the Spirit of Forgiveness; that where there is discord, I may bring Harmony; that where there is error, I may bring Truth; that where there is doubt, I may bring Faith; that where there is despair, I may bring Hope; that where there are shadows, I may bring Light; that where there is sadness, I may bring Joy.

Lord, grant that I may seek rather to comfort, than to be comforted, to understand, than to be understood, to love, than to be loved, for it is by forgetting self that one finds, it is by forgiving that one is forgiven, it is by dying that one awakens to eternal life.

— ADAPTED FROM THE PRAYER OF SAINT FRANCIS

Miss no single opportunity of making some small sacrifice, here by a smiling look, there by a kindly word; always doing the smallest right and doing it all for love.

— SAINT THERESE OF LISIEUX

I assure you, as often as you did it for one of the least of my brothers, you did it to me.

— JESUS, MATTHEW 25:40 NAB

On Jesus

Jesus is the truth that must be shared.

— MOTHER TERESA

Very truly, I tell you, the one who believes in me will also do the works that I do, in fact, will do greater works than these. If in my name you ask for anything, I will do it.

— JESUS, JOHN 14:12-14 RSV

There is a story of a little robin. He saw Jesus on the cross, saw the crown of thorns. The bird flew around and around until he found a way to remove a thorn, and in removing the thorn stuck himself.

Each one of us should be that bird. What have I done? What comfort have I given? Does my work really mean something? The little robin tried to remove just one thorn. When I look at the cross, I think of that robin. Don't pass by the cross; it is a place of grace.

We often look without seeing. Am I able to see the poor and suffering? All of us have to carry our own cross, all of us have to accompany Jesus in His ascent to Calvary if we want to reach the summit with Him. Sacrifice, in order to be genuine, has to empty us of ourselves. Jesus has chosen each one of us to be His love and His light in the world.

Remember, He has chosen us; we have not first chosen Him. We must respond by making something beautiful for God — something very beautiful. For this we must give our all, our utmost. We must cling to Jesus, grasp Him, have a grip on Him, and never let go for anything. We must fall in love with Jesus.

By my vow of chastity, I not only renounce the married state of life, but I also consecrate to God the free use of my internal and external acts, my affections. I cannot in conscience love another with the love of a woman for a man. I no longer have the right to give that affection to any other creature but only to God.

What, then? Do we have to be stones, human beings without hearts? Do we simply say, "I don't care; to me all human beings are the same"? No, not at all. We have to keep ourselves as we are, but keep it all for God, to whom we have consecrated all our external and internal acts.

Chastity does not simply mean that I am not married. It means that I love Christ with an undivided love. It is something deeper, something living, something real. It is to love Him with undivided, loving chastity through the freedom of poverty.

The words of Jesus, "Love one another as I have loved you," (John 15:12 RSV) must be not only a light for us but a flame that consumes the self in us. Love, in order to survive, must be nourished by sacrifices, especially the sacrifice of self. Renouncing means to offer my free will, my reason, my life, in an attitude of faith. My soul can be in darkness; trials are the surest tests of my blind renunciation. Renunciation also means love. The more we renounce, the more we love God and man.

Am I convinced of Christ's love for me and mine for Him? This conviction is like a sunlight that makes the sap of life rise and the buds of sanctity bloom. This conviction is the rock on which sanctity is built. What must we do to get this conviction? We must know Jesus, love Jesus, serve Jesus. We know Him through prayers, meditations, and spiritual duties. We love Him through holy Mass and the sacraments and through that intimate union of love. We must endeavor to live alone with Him in the sanctuary of our inmost heart.

In his passion our Lord says, "Thy will be done. Do with me what you want." And that was the hardest thing for our Lord even at the last moment. They say that the passion in Gethsemane was much greater than even the crucifixion. Because it was His heart, His soul that was being crucified, while on the cross, it was His body that was crucified. And the only way that we know that it was so difficult for Him that hour is that He asked, "Why could you not spend one hour with me?" We know He needed consolation. This is total surrender — not to be loved by anybody, not to be wanted by anybody, just to be a nobody because we have given all to Christ.

When Jesus came into the world, He loved it so much that He gave His life for it. He wanted to satisfy our hunger for God. And what did He do? He made Himself the Bread of Life. He became small, fragile, and defenseless for us. Bits of bread can be so small that even a baby can chew it, even a dying person can eat it. He became the Bread of Life to satisfy our hunger for God, our hunger for love.

I don't think we could have ever loved God if Jesus had not become one of us. So that we might be able to love God, He became one of us in all things, except sin. If we have been created in the image of God, then we have been created to love, because God is love. In his passion Jesus taught us how to forgive out of love, how to forget out of humility. Find Jesus, and you will find peace.

Don't allow anything to interfere with your love for Jesus. You belong to Him. Nothing can separate you from Him. That one sentence is important to remember. He will be your joy, your strength. If you hold onto that sentence, temptations and difficulties will come, but nothing will break you. Remember, you have been created for great things.

You must not be afraid to say "Yes" to Jesus, because there is no greater love than His love and no greater joy than His joy. My prayer for you is that you come to understand and have the courage to answer Jesus' call to you with the simple word, "Yes." Why has He chosen you? Why me? This is a mystery.

Christ said, "I was hungry and you gave me food." He was hungry not only for bread but for the understanding love of being loved, of being known, of being someone to someone. He was naked not only of clothing but of human dignity and of respect, through the injustice that is done to the poor, who are looked down upon simply because they are poor. He was dispossessed not only of a house made of bricks but because of the dispossession of those who are locked up, of those who are unwanted and unloved, of those who walk through the world with no one to care for them.

You may go out into the street and have nothing to say, but maybe there is a man standing there on the corner and you go to him. Maybe he resents you, but you are there, and that presence is there. You must radiate that presence that is within you, in the way you address that man with love and respect. Why? Because you believe that is Jesus. Jesus cannot receive you — for this, you must know how to go to Him. He comes disguised in the form of that person there. Jesus, in the least of His brethren, is not only hungry for a piece of bread, but hungry for love, to be known, to be taken into account.

What is my spiritual life? A love union with Jesus in which the divine and the human give themselves completely to one another. All that Jesus asks of me is to give myself to Him in all my poverty and nothingness.

Jesus said, "Learn of me." In our meditations we should always say, "Jesus, make me a saint according to your own heart, meek and humble." We must respond in the spirit in which Jesus meant us to respond. We know Him better through meditations, and the study of the gospel, but have we really understood Him in His humility?

One thing Jesus asks of me: that I lean on Him; that in Him and only in Him I put complete trust; that I surrender myself to Him unreservedly. Even when all goes wrong and I feel as if I am a ship without a compass, I must give myself completely to Him. I must not attempt to control God's action; I must not count the stages in the journey He would have me make. I must not desire a clear perception of my advance upon the road, must not know precisely where I am upon the way of holiness. I ask Him to make a saint of me, yet I must leave to Him the choice of the saintliness itself and still more the means that lead to it.

Hungry for love, He looks at you.
Thirsty for kindness, He begs from you.
Naked for loyalty, He hopes in you.
Sick and imprisoned for friendship, He wants from you.
Homeless for shelter in your heart, He asks of you.
Will you be that one to Him?

The simplicity of our life of contemplation makes us see the face of God in everything, everyone, and everywhere, all the time. His hand in all happenings makes us do all that we do — whether we think, study, work, speak, eat, or take our rest —

in Jesus, with Jesus, for Jesus and to Jesus, under the loving gaze of the Father, being totally available to Him in any form He may come to us.

I am deeply impressed by the fact that before explaining the Word of God, before presenting to the crowds the eight beatitudes, Jesus had compassion on them and gave them food. Only then did He begin to teach them.

Love Jesus generously. Love him trustfully, without looking back and without fear. Give yourself fully to Jesus, He will use you to accomplish great things on the condition that you believe much more in His love than in your weakness. Believe in Him, trust in Him with a blind and absolute confidence because He is Jesus. Believe that Jesus and Jesus alone is life, and sanctity is nothing but that same Jesus intimately living in you; then His hand will be free with you.

Who is Jesus to me?

Jesus is the Word made flesh.

Jesus is the Bread of Life.

Jesus is the Victim offered for our sins on the cross.

Jesus is the sacrifice offered at holy Mass for the sins of the world and for mine.

Jesus is the Word to be spoken.

Jesus is the truth to be told.

Jesus is the way to be walked.

Jesus is the light to be lit.

Jesus is the life to be lived.

Jesus is the love to be loved.

Jesus is the joy to be shared.

Jesus is the peace to be given.

Jesus is the hungry to be fed.

Jesus is the thirsty to be satiated.

Jesus is the naked to be clothed.

Jesus is the homeless to be taken in.

Jesus is the sick to be healed.

Jesus is the lonely to be loved.

Jesus is the unwanted to be wanted.

Jesus is the leper to wash His wounds.

Jesus is the beggar to give Him a smile.

Jesus is the drunkard to listen to Him.

Jesus is the mentally ill to protect Him.

Jesus is the little one to embrace Him.

Jesus is the blind to lead Him.

Jesus is the dumb to speak for Him.

Jesus is the crippled to walk with Him.

Jesus is the drug addict to befriend Him.

Jesus is the prostitute to remove from danger and befriend I ler.

Jesus is the prisoner to be visited.

Jesus is the old to be served.

To me: Jesus is my God.

Jesus is my spouse.

Jesus is my life.

Jesus is my only love.

Jesus is my all in all.

Jesus is my everything.

JESUS, I love with my whole heart, with my whole being. I have given Him all, even my sins, and He has espoused me to Himself in all tenderness and love.

I am no longer my own. Whether I live or whether I die, I belong to my Saviour. I have nothing of my own. God is my all, and my whole being is His.

I will have nothing to do with a love that would be for God or in God. I cannot bear the word for or the word in, because they denote something that may be in between God and me.

— Saint Catherine of Genoa

As the Father has loved me, so I have loved you; abide in my love. If you keep my commandments, you will abide in my love, just as I have kept my Father's commandments and abide in His love. I have said these things so that my joy may be in you, and that your joy may be complete.

— Jesus, John 15:9-11 RSV

On Poverty & the Poor

God has not created poverty; it is we who have created it. Before God, all of us are poor.

— MOTHER TERESA

Blessed are the poor in spirit, for theirs is the kingdom of heaven.

— JESUS, MATTHEW 5:3 RSV

Poverty doesn't only consist of being hungry for bread, but rather it is a tremendous hunger for human dignity. We need to love and to be somebody for someone else. This is where we make our mistake and shove people aside. Not only have we denied the poor a piece of bread, but by thinking that they have no worth and leaving them abandoned in the streets, we have denied them the human dignity that is rightfully theirs as children of God.

The world today is hungry not only for bread but hungry for love, hungry to be wanted, to be loved. They're hungry to feel the presence of Christ. In many countries, people have everything except that presence, that understanding.

In every country there are poor. On certain continents poverty is more spiritual than material, a poverty that consists of loneliness, discouragement, and the lack of meaning in life. I have also seen in Europe and America very poor people sleeping on newspapers or rags in the streets. There are those kind of poor in London, Madrid, and Rome. It is too easy simply to talk or concern ourselves with the poor who are far away. It is much harder and, perhaps, more challenging to turn our attention and concern toward the poor who live right next door to us.

When I pick up a hungry person from the streets, I give him rice and bread, and I have satisfied that hunger. But a person who is shut out, feels unwanted by society, unloved and terrified — how much more difficult is it to remove that hunger?

You in the West have the spiritually poorest of the poor much more than you have the physically poor. Often among the rich are very spiritually poor people. I find it is easy to give a plate of rice to a hungry person, to furnish a bed to a person who has no bed, but to console or to remove the bitterness, anger, and loneliness that comes from being spiritually deprived, that takes a long time.

❧

From all parts of the world young people are coming to India to take on a very poor life, poorer than ours. They are driven by the desire to be free from their environment of wealth. I think they want to be living examples of Christ's poverty. It is not enough to know the spirit of poverty, you have to know poverty itself. Poverty means not having anything. Today, everyone, even those who come from well-to-do environments, wants to know what it really means to have nothing.

Riches, both material and spiritual, can choke you if you do not use them fairly. For not even God can put anything in a heart that is already full. One day there springs up the desire for money and for all that money can provide — the superfluous, luxury in eating, luxury in dressing, trifles. Needs increase because one thing calls for another. The result is uncontrollable dissatisfaction. Let us remain as empty as possible so that God can fill us up.

Our Lord gives us a living example: From the very first day of His human existence He was brought up in a poverty which no human being will ever be able to experience, because "being rich He made Himself poor." Christ being rich emptied Himself. This is where the contradiction lies. If I want to be poor like Christ, who became poor even though He was rich, I must do the same. It would be a shame for us to be richer than Jesus, who for our sake endured poverty.

On the cross Christ was deprived of everything. The cross itself had been given Him by Pilate; nails and the crown, by the soldiers. He was naked. When He died He was stripped of the cross, the nails, and the crown. He was wrapped in a piece of canvas donated by a charitable soul, and He was buried in a tomb that did not belong to Him. Despite all that, Jesus could have died like a king and could even have been spared death. He chose poverty because He knew that it was the genuine means to possess God and to bring His love to the earth.

Poverty is freedom. It is a freedom so that what I possess doesn't own me, so that what I possess doesn't hold me down, so that my possessions don't keep me from sharing or giving of myself.

Rigorous poverty is our safeguard. We do not want, as has been the case with other religious orders throughout history, to begin serving the poor and then gradually move toward serving the rich. In order for us to understand and to be able to help those who lack everything, we have to live as they live. The difference lies only in the fact that those we aid are poor by force, whereas we are poor by choice.

A few weeks ago, I picked up a child from the street, and from the face I could see that little child was hungry. I didn't know how many days that little one had not eaten. So I gave her a piece of bread, and the little one took the bread and, crumb by crumb, started eating it. I said to her, "Eat, eat the bread. You are hungry." And the little one looked at me and said, "I am afraid. When the bread will be finished, I will be hungry again."

We have no right to judge the rich. For our part, what we desire is not a class struggle but a class encounter, in which the rich save the poor and the poor save the rich.

With regard to God, our poverty is our humble recognition and acceptance of our sinfulness, helplessness, and utter nothingness, and the acknowledgment of our neediness before Him, which expresses itself as hope in Him, as an openness to receive all things from Him as from our Father. Our poverty should be true gospel poverty: gentle, tender, glad, and openhearted, always ready to give an expression of love. Poverty is love before it is renunciation. To love, it is necessary to give. To give, it is necessary to be free from selfishness.

Poverty is necessary because we are working with the poor. When they complain about the food, we can say, we eat the same. They say, "It was so hot last night, we could not sleep." We can reply, "We also felt very hot." The poor have to wash for themselves, go barefoot; we do the same. We have to go down and lift them up. It opens the heart of the poor when we can say we live the same way they do. Sometimes they only have one bucket of water. It is the same with us. The poor have to stand in line; we do too. Food, clothing, everything must be like that of the poor. We have no fasting. Our fasting is to eat the food as we get it.

Our lives, to be fruitful, must be full of Christ; to be able to bring His peace, joy, and love we must have it ourselves, for we cannot give what we have not got — the blind leading the blind. The poor in the slums are without Jesus and we have the privilege of entering their homes. What they think of us does not matter, but what we are to them does matter. To go to the slums merely for the sake of going will not be enough to draw them to Jesus. If we are preoccupied with ourselves and our own affairs, we will not be able to live up to this ideal.

We practice the virtue of poverty when we mend our clothes quickly and as beautifully as we can. Patched clothes are no disgrace. It is said of Saint Francis of Assisi that when he died his habit had so many patches that the original cloth was no longer there.

The gospels remind us that Jesus, before He taught the people, felt compassion for the multitudes that followed after Him. Sometimes He felt it even to the point of forgetting to eat. How did He put

His compassion into practice? He multiplied the loaves of bread and the fish to satisfy their hunger. He gave them food to eat until they couldn't eat any more, and twelve basketfuls were left over. Then He taught them. Only then did He tell them the Good News. This is what we must often do in our work: We must first satisfy the needs of the body, so we can then bring Christ to the poor.

Jesus gives me the opportunity to feed Him by feeding those who are hungry, to clothe Him by clothing those who are naked, to heal Him by caring for those who are sick, and to offer Him shelter by housing those who are homeless and unwanted.

I remember the day I picked up a woman in the street, thinking that she was starving to death. I offered her a dish of rice. She kept looking at it for a long while. I tried to persuade her to eat. Then she said, with utter simplicity, "I can't believe it's rice. I have been a long time without eating." She condemned no one. She did not complain against the rich. She did not utter any bitter words. She simply couldn't believe it was rice.

∽

We know what that poverty means, first of all, to be hungry for bread, to need clothing, and to not have a home. But there is a far greater kind of poverty. It means being unwanted, unloved, and neglected. It means having no one to call your own.

Do we know our poor people? Do we know the poor in our house, in our family? Perhaps they are not hungry for a piece of bread. Perhaps our children, husband, wife, are not hungry, or naked, or dispossessed, but are you sure there is no one there who feels unwanted, deprived of affection? Where is your elderly father or mother? Abandonment is an awful poverty.

There are lonely people around you in hospitals and psychiatric wards. There are so many people that are homeless! In New York, our sisters are working among the destitute who are dying. What pain it causes to see these people! They are only known by their street address now. Yet they were all someone's children. Someone loved them at one time. They loved others during their lifetime. But now they are only known by their street address.

Know the poorest of the poor are among your neighbors, in your neighborhoods, in your town, in your city, perhaps in your own family. When you know them, that will lead you to love them. And love will impel you to serve them. Only then will you begin to act like Jesus and live out the gospel. Place yourselves at the service of the poor. Open your hearts to love them. Be living witnesses of God's mercy.

The poor do not need our compassion or our pity; they need our help. What they give to us is more than what we give to them.

The poor are wonderful people. They have their own dignity, which we can easily see. Usually the poor are not known, and therefore one is not able to discover their dignity. But the poor have above all great courage to lead the life they lead. They are forced to live like that; poverty has been imposed on them. We choose poverty; they are forced to accept it.

The poor are our prayer. They carry God in themselves. God created the world and saw that it was good. God created man and saw that he was good. God created everything, and He realized that each thing was good. How can we complain against God for the poverty and suffering that exist in the world? Can we honestly do so? God saw that everything was good. What we do with things is another matter.

In order to help us deserve heaven, Christ set a condition: At the moment of our death, you and I, whoever we might have been and wherever we have lived, Christians and non-Christians alike, every human being who has been created by the loving hand of God in His own image, shall stand in His presence and be judged according to what we have been for the poor, what we have done for them. Here a beautiful standard for judgment presents itself. We have to become increasingly aware that the poor are the hope of humanity, for we will be judged by how we have treated the poor. We will have to face this reality when we are summoned before the throne of God: "I was hungry. I was naked. I was homeless. And whatever you did to the least of my brethren, you did it to me."

When we recognize that our suffering neighbor

is the image of God Himself, and when we understand the consequences of that truth, poverty will no longer exist and we, the Missionaries of Charity, will no longer have any work to do.

Christ chose to appear despised, needy, and poor in this world, so that people who were in utter poverty might become rich in Him by possessing the kingdom of heaven. Rejoice and be glad.

— SAINT CLARE OF ASSISI

For who is greater, the one who is at the table or the one who serves? Is it not the one at the table? But I am among you as one who serves.

— JESUS, LUKE 22:27 RSV

On Forgiveness

Every human being comes from the hand of God, and we all know something of God's love for us. Whatever our religion, we know that if we really want to love, we must first learn to forgive before anything else.

— MOTHER TERESA

. . . and forgive us the wrong we have done as we forgive those who wrong us.

— JESUS, MATTHEW 6:12 NAB

W e have opened a home in New York for AIDS patients, who find themselves among the most unwanted people of today. What a tremendous change has been brought about in their lives just because of a few sisters who take care of them and have made a home for them. A place, perhaps the only place, where they feel loved, where they are somebody to someone. This has changed their lives in such a way that they die a most beautiful death. Not one of them has yet died in distress.

The other day, a sister called to tell me that one of the young men was dying but, strange to say, he couldn't die. So she asked him, "What is wrong?"

And he said, "Sister, I cannot die until I ask my father to forgive me." So the sister found out where the father was, and she called him. And something extraordinary happened, like a living page from the gospel: The father embraced his son and cried, "My son! My beloved son!" And the son begged the father, "Forgive me! Forgive me!" And the two of them clung to each other tenderly. Hours later, the young man died.

When we realize that we are all sinners needing forgiveness, it will be easy for us to forgive others. We have to be forgiven in order to be able to forgive. If I do not understand this, it will be very hard for me to say "I forgive you" to anyone who comes to me.

Confession is a beautiful act of great love. Only in confession can we go as sinners with sin and come out as sinners without sin.

Confession is nothing but humility in action. We used to call it penance, but really it is a sacrament of love, a sacrament of forgiveness. When there is a gap between me and Christ, when my love is divided, anything can come to fill the gap. Confession is a place where I allow Jesus to take away from me everything that divides, that destroys.

The reality of my sins must come first. For most of us there is the danger of forgetting that we are sinners and must go to confession as sinners. We must go to God to tell Him we are sorry for all we have done that may have hurt Him.

The confessional is not a place for useless conversation or gossip. The topic should be my sins, my sorrow, my forgiveness; how to overcome my temptations, how to practice virtue, how to increase in the love of God.

Penance is absolutely necessary. Nothing is of greater force in restraining the disordered passions of the soul and in subjecting the natural appetites to right reason. Through penance we come to possess those heavenly joys and delights that surpass the pleasures of earth as much as the soul does the body, and heaven the earth.

Our penance is an act of perfect love of God, man, and the whole universe. It is for us a joyful identification with Christ crucified; it is a hunger to be lost in Him, so that nothing remains of us but He alone in His radiant glory drawing all men to the Father.

The other day, a man, a journalist, asked me a strange question. He asked me, "Even you, do you have to go to confession?" I said, "Yes, I go to confession every week." And he said, "Then God must be very demanding if you have to go to confession." And I said, "Your own child sometimes does something wrong. What happens when your child comes to you and says, 'Daddy, I'm sorry'? What do you do? You put both of your arms around your child and kiss him. Why? Because that's your way of telling him that you love him. God does the same thing. He loves you tenderly." Even when we sin or make a mistake, let's allow that to help us grow closer to God. Let's tell Him humbly, "I know I shouldn't have done this, but even this failure I offer to you."

If we have sinned or made a mistake, let us go to Him and say, "I'm sorry! I repent." God is a forgiving Father. His mercy is greater than our sins.

He will forgive us.

This is humility: to have the courage to accept humiliation and receive God's forgiveness. Our souls should be like a transparent crystal through which God can be perceived.

Our crystal is sometimes covered with dirt and dust. To remove this dust we carry out an examination of our conscience in order to obtain a clean heart. God will help us to remove that dust, as long as we allow Him to; if that is our will, His will comes about.

Perhaps this is what we have lacked. Our examination of our conscience is the mirror we focus toward nature: a human test, no doubt, but one that needs a mirror in order to faithfully reflect its faults. If we undertake this task with greater faithfulness, perhaps we will realize that what we sometimes consider a stumbling block is rather a rock we can step on. The knowledge of our sin helps us to rise.

Knowledge of self is very necessary for confession. That is why the saints could say they were wicked criminals. They saw God and then saw themselves, and they saw the difference. We become hurt because we do not know ourselves, and our eyes are not fixed on God alone; so we do not have real knowledge of God. When the saints looked upon themselves with such horror, they really meant it. They were not pretending.

Knowledge of ourselves will help us to rise up, whereas sin and weakness will lead to despondency. Deep confidence and trust will come through self-knowledge. Then you will turn to Jesus to support you in your weakness, whereas if you think you are strong, you will not need our Lord.

Reconciliation begins with ourselves. It begins with a pure heart, a heart that is able to see God in others.

In the Constitution of the Missionaries of Charity, we have a beautiful part that speaks of the tenderness of Christ, and also of his faithful friendship and love. To make that love more living, more sure, more tender, Jesus gives us the Eucharist. This is why it is necessary for every Missionary of Charity to feed upon the Eucharist in order to be a true carrier of God's love. She must live on the Eucharist and have her heart and life woven with the Eucharist. No Missionary of Charity can give Jesus if she does not have Jesus in her heart.

Our life is linked to the Eucharist. Through faith in and love of the body of Christ under the appearance of bread, we take Christ literally: "I was hungry and you gave me food. I was a stranger and you welcomed me, naked and you clothed me."

The Eucharist is connected with the passion. I was giving Communion this morning — my two fingers were holding Jesus. Try to realize that Jesus allows Himself to be broken.

The Eucharist involves more than just receiving; it also involves satisfying the hunger of Christ. He says, "Come to me." He is hungry for souls. Nowhere does the gospel say, "Go away," but always, "Come to me." Ask Jesus to be with you, to work with you that you may be able to pray the work. You must really be sure that you have received Jesus. After that, you cannot give your tongue, your thoughts, or your heart to bitterness.

For us, we must never separate the Eucharist and the poor or the poor and the Eucharist. He satisfied my hunger for Him and now I go to satisfy His hunger for souls, for love.

The Eucharist is the sacrament of prayer, the fountain and summit of Christian life. Our Eucharist is incomplete if it does not lead us to service and love for the poor.

Someone could ask, "Who are the poorest of the poor?" They are the unwanted, the unloved, the uncared for, the hungry, the forgotten, the naked, the homeless, the lepers, the alcoholics. But also we Missionaries of Charity are the poorest of the poor. To be able to work, to be able to see, to be able to love, we need this Eucharistic union.

When we remember that every morning at Communion we have held in our hands all the holiness of God, we feel more willing to abstain from everything that may stain our purity. Thence flows a sincere and deep respect for our own person — respect also toward others leading us to treat them with sensitivity but likewise abstaining from all disordered sentimentality.

Holy Communion, as the word itself implies, is the intimate union of Jesus and our soul and body. The saints understood so well that they could spend hours in preparation and still more in thanksgiving. This needs no explanation, for who could explain "the depth of the riches of the wisdom and knowledge of God"? "How incomprehensible are His judgments!" cried Saint Paul, "And how unsearchable His ways, for who has known the mind of the Lord?"

If you really want to grow in love, come back to the Eucharist and let us often say during the day, "Lord, wash away my sins and cleanse me from all my iniquity."

Christ made Himself the Bread of Life. He wanted to give Himself to us in a very special way, in a simple, tangible way, because it is hard for human beings to love a God whom they cannot see.

If the greatest sinner on earth should repent at the moment of death, and draw his last breath in an act of love, neither the many graces he has abused, nor the many sins he has committed would stand in his way. Our Lord would receive Him into His mercy.

— SAINT THERESE OF LISIEUX

So when you are offering your gift at the altar, if you remember that your brother or sister has something against you, leave your gift there before the altar and go; first be reconciled to your brother or sister, and then come and offer your gift.

— JESUS, MATTHEW 5:23-24 RSV

On Children & the Family

☙

I will take any child, any time, night or day. Just let me know and I will come for him.

— MOTHER TERESA

Let the little children come to me: Do not stop them; for it is to such as these that the kingdom of God belongs.

— JESUS, MARK 10:14 RSV

I have a conviction that I want to share with you. Love begins at home, and every Co-worker* should try to make sure that deep family love abides in his or her home. Only when love abides at home can we share it with our next-door neighbor. Then it will show forth and you will be able to say to them, "Yes, love is here." And then you will be able to share it with everyone around you.

One day I found a little girl in the street, so I took her to our children's home. We have a nice place and good food there. We gave her clean

---

*See pages 200 and 205 for more information about the Co-workers.

clothes and we made her as happy as we could.

After a few hours, the little girl ran away. I looked for her, but I couldn't find her anywhere. Then after a few days, I found her again. And, again, I brought her to our home and told a sister, "Sister, please, follow this child wherever she goes."

The little girl ran away again. But the sister followed to find out where she was going and why she kept running away.

She followed the little girl and discovered that the little one's mother was living under a tree in the street. The mother had placed two stones there and did her cooking under that tree.

The sister sent word to me and I went there. I found joy on that little girl's face, because she was with her mother, who loved her and was making special food for her in that little open place.

I asked the little girl, "How is it that you would not stay with us? You had so many beautiful things in our home."

She answered, "I could not live without my mother. She loves me." That little girl was happier to have the meager food her mother was cooking in the street than all the things I had given her.

While the child was with us, I could scarcely see a smile on her face. But when I found her there with her mother, in the street, they were smiling.

Why? Because they were family.

Right from the beginning, since love begins at home, I think we should teach our children to love one another at home. I think this will strengthen our children, so that they can give that love to others in the future.

I cannot remember now in what city I was, but I do remember that I did not see any children on the street. I missed the children very badly. While I was walking down the street, suddenly I saw a baby carriage. A young woman was pushing the carriage, and I crossed the street just to see the child. To my terrible surprise, there was no child in the carriage. There was a little dog! Apparently the hunger in the heart of that woman had to be satisfied. So, not having a child, she looked for a substitute. She found a dog. I love dogs myself very much, but still I cannot bear seeing a dog given the place of a child.

People are afraid of having children. Children have lost their place in the family. Children are so very, very lonely! When children come home from school, there is no one to greet them. Then they go back to the streets. We must find our children again and bring them back home. Mothers are at the heart of the family. Children need their mothers. If the mother is there, the children will be there too. For the family to be whole, the children and the mother also need the father to be present in the home. I think if we can help to bring them all back together, we will be doing a beautiful thing for God.

We are here to be witnesses of love and to celebrate life, because life has been created in the image of God. Life is to love and to be loved. That is why we all have to take a strong stand so that no child, boy or girl, will be rejected or unloved. Every child is a sign of God's love, that has to be extended over all the earth.

If you hear of someone who does not want to have her child, who wants to have an abortion, try to convince her to bring the child to me. I will love that child, who is a sign of God's love.

I don't want to talk about what should be legal or illegal. I don't think any human heart should dare to take life, or any human hand be raised to destroy life. Life is the life of God in us. Life is the greatest gift that God has bestowed on human beings, and man has been created in the image of God. Life belongs to God, and we have no right to destroy it.

As soon as Mary received the announcement from the angel, she went in haste to her cousin Elizabeth, who was with child. And the unborn child, John the Baptist, rejoiced in Elizabeth's womb. How wonderful it was — Almighty God chose an unborn child to announce the coming of His Son!

Mary, in the mystery of her annunciation and visitation, is the very model of the way we should live, because first she received Jesus in her life; then what she had received, she had to share. In every Holy Communion, Jesus the Word becomes flesh in our life — a special, delicate, beautiful gift of God.

This was the first Eucharist: the gift of His son establishing in her the first altar. Mary, the only one who was able to affirm with complete sincerity, "This is my body," from that moment on, offered her body, her strength, her whole being, to form the body of Christ.

Our mother the Church has elevated women to a great honor in the presence of God by proclaiming Mary the mother of the Church.

When we were invited to take care of the young women of Bangladesh who had been raped by soldiers, we saw the need to open a home for children. The difficulties were great because accepting in society young women who had been raped went against both Hindu and Muslim laws. But when the leader of Bangladesh said that those young women were heroines of the nation, who had fought for their own purity, who had struggled for their country, their very parents came to look for them. Some people favored abortion. I told the government that the young women had been violated, whereas what they wanted to do was force these women or help them commit a transgression that would accompany them throughout their lives. Thanks be to God, the government accepted our conditions that each of the children for whom abortion would have been chosen should be taken to the house of Mother Teresa to receive help. Of the forty children we received, more than thirty went to Canada and other countries, adopted by generous families.

I believe that the cry of the children, those who are never born because they are killed before they see the light of day, must offend God greatly.

We asked God to send us someone to help women cope with their difficulties with a clear conscience, a healthy body, and in a happy family. There came to us a sister from Mauritius Island who had attended a course on family planning.

Right now there are more than three thousand families who use natural family planning, and it has been about 95 percent effective. When people see these good effects in their families, they come to us to say thanks. Some of them have said, "Our family has stayed together, in good health, and we have a child when we desire it."

I think if we could bring this method to every country, if our poor people would learn it, there would be more peace, more love in the family between parents and children.

People very often make jokes with me (or about me, rather), because we are teaching natural family planning. They say, "Mother Teresa is doing plenty of talking about family planning, but she herself does not practice it. She is having more and more children every day."

Indeed, that is the way it is. Our homes are always full of children. And as they come, God has been tremendously wonderful to us. You would be surprised how much love is showered on those unwanted little children, who otherwise would have been destined to live in the gutter.

I think the world today is upside-down. It is

suffering so much because there is so little love in the home and in family life. We have no time for our children. We have no time for each other. There is no time to enjoy each other, and the lack of love causes so much suffering and unhappiness in the world.

Are we able to perceive the needs of our children? Do our children come home with us, as Jesus went home with Mary His mother? Do we offer our children a home?

When our children are pulled away from us and receive bad advice, do we feel that deep tenderness that makes us go after them in order to draw them toward us, to welcome them kindly in our home, and to love them with all our heart?

Everybody today seems to be in such a terrible rush, anxious for greater development and greater riches. Children have very little time for their parents and parents have very little time for their children and for each other. So the breakdown of peace in the world begins at home.

Bring prayer to your family, bring it to your

little children. Teach them to pray. For a child that prays is a happy child. A family that prays is a united family. We hear of so many broken families. And then we examine them: Why are they broken? I think because they never pray together. They are never in prayer before the Lord.

I cannot forget my mother. She was usually very busy all day long. But when sunset drew near, it was her custom to hurry with her tasks in order to be ready to receive my father. At the time we did not understand, and we would smile and even joke a little about it. Today I cannot help but call to mind that great delicacy of love that she had for him. No matter what happened, she was always prepared, with a smile on her lips, to welcome him.

Today we have no time. Fathers and mothers are so busy that when children come home they are not welcomed with love or with a smile.

If we help our children to be what they should be today, then, when tomorrow becomes today, they will have the necessary courage to face it with greater love. From the very beginning, since love begins at home, I think we should teach our children to love one another. They can learn this only from their father and mother, when they see the parents' love for each other. I think this will strengthen our children, so that they can give that love to others in the future.

People who really and truly love each other are the happiest people in the world. We see that with our very poor people. They love their children and they love their families. They may have very little, in fact, they may not have anything, but they are happy people.

Jesus was born into a family and stayed in Nazareth for thirty years. He had come to redeem the world, yet He spent thirty years in Nazareth, doing the humble work of an ordinary person. He spent all those years just living out family life.

A child is the greatest of God's gifts to a family, because it is the fruit of the parents' love.

If you want a happy family, if you want a holy family, give your hearts to love.

— MOTHER TERESA

Many children came to see Jesus, and the apostles said to them, "Don't come!" But Jesus said, "Let the children come to me. I love them."

Neither can they die any more: for they are equal unto the angels, and are the children of God, being the children of the resurrection.

— LUKE 20:36 KJV

On Suffering & Death

The prize with which God rewards our self-abandonment is Himself.

— MOTHER TERESA

Come to me, all you that are weary and are carrying heavy burdens, and I will give you rest.

Take my yoke upon you, and learn from me; for I am gentle and humble in heart, and you will find rest for your souls. For my yoke is easy, and my burden is light.

— JESUS, MATTHEW 11:28-30 RSV

My thoughts often run to you who suffer, and
I offer your sufferings, which are so great,
while mine are so small.

Those of you who are sick, when things are
hard, take refuge in Christ's heart. There my own
heart will find with you strength and love.

Often, when my work is very hard, I think
about my sick Co-workers and say to Jesus, "Look
at these children of yours who suffer, and bless my
work for their sake." I feel instantly comforted. You
see, they are our hidden treasure, the secret strength
of the Missionaries of Charity. I personally feel very
happy, and a new strength comes over my soul, as I

think of those who are spiritually united to us.

Recently a real windfall of charity was experienced throughout Bengal. Food and clothing arrived from everywhere. It came from schools, men, women, and children, to be distributed during the monsoon disaster. The monsoon was something terrible, but it brought about something very beautiful. It brought about sharing. It brought about the concern and awareness that our brothers and sisters were suffering because of a natural disaster. And many people decided to do something to help them. There were people who prepared meals in their homes to share with those in need. It was something very beautiful to witness that such terrible suffering could help bring about so much good in so many people.

Suffering will never be completely absent from our lives. So don't be afraid of suffering. Your suffering is a great means of love, if you make use of it, especially if you offer it for peace in the world. Suffering in and of itself is useless, but suffering that is shared with the passion of Christ is a wonderful gift and a sign of love. Christ's suffering proved to be a gift, the greatest gift of love, because through his suffering our sins were atoned for.

Suffering, pain, sorrow, humiliation, feelings of loneliness, are nothing but the kiss of Jesus, a sign that you have come so close that He can kiss you.

Remember that the passion of Christ ends always in the joy of the resurrection of Christ, so when you feel in your own heart the suffering of Christ, remember the resurrection has to come. Never let anything so fill you with sorrow as to make you forget the joy of Christ risen.

In twenty-five years, we have picked up more than thirty-six thousand people from the streets and more than eighteen thousand have died a most beautiful death.

When we pick them up from the street we give them a plate of rice. In no time we revive them. A few nights ago we picked up four people. One was in a most terrible condition, covered with wounds, full of maggots. I told the sisters that I would take care of her while they attended to the other three. I really did all that my love could do for her. I put her in bed and then she took hold of my hand. She had such a beautiful smile on her face and she said only, "Thank you." Then she died.

There was a greatness of love. She was hungry for love, and she received that love before she died. She spoke only two words, but her understanding love was expressed in those two words.

In New York we have a home for AIDS patients who are dying from what I call "the leprosy of the West." On Christmas Eve, I opened this house as a gift to Jesus for His birthday. We started with fifteen beds for some poor AIDS patients and four young men I brought out of jail because they didn't want to die there. They were our first guests. I made a little chapel for them. There these young people who had not been near Jesus could come back to Him if they wanted to. Thanks to God's blessing and His love, their hearts completely changed.

Once when I went there, one of them had to go

to the hospital. He said to me, "Mother Teresa, you are my friend. I want to speak to you alone." So the sisters went out, and he spoke. And what did this man say? This was someone who hadn't been to confession or received Holy Communion in twenty-five years. In all those years, he had had nothing to do with Jesus. He told me, "You know, Mother Teresa, when I get a terrible headache, I compare it with the pain that Jesus had when they crowned Him with thorns. When I get that terrible pain in my back, I compare it with Jesus' when He was scourged. When I get that terrible pain in my hands and feet, I compare it with the pain Jesus had when they crucified Him. I ask you to take me back home. I want to die with you."

I got permission from the doctor to take him back home with me. I took him to the chapel. I have never seen anybody talk to God the way that young man talked to him. There was such an understanding love between Jesus and him. After three days, he died.

It is hard to understand the change that young man experienced. What brought it about? Perhaps it was the tender love the sisters gave him that made him understand God loved him.

As Christians, we have been created for great things. We have been created to be holy since we have been created in the image of God. For that reason, when someone dies that person is meant to go home to God. That is where we are all meant to go.

Something happened to one of our sisters who was sent to study. The day she was to receive her degree, she died. As she was dying she asked, "Why did Jesus call me for such a short time?" And her superior answered, "Jesus wants you, not your works." She was perfectly happy after that.

At the moment of death, we will not be judged by the amount of work we have done but by the weight of love we have put into our work. This love should flow from self-sacrifice, and it must be felt to the point of hurting.

Death, in the final analysis, is only the easiest and quickest means to go back to God. If only we could make people understand that we come from God and that we have to go back to Him!

Death is the most decisive moment in human life. It is like our coronation: to die in peace with God.

Death can be something beautiful. It is like going home. He who dies in God goes home even though we naturally miss the person who has gone. But it is something beautiful. That person has gone home to God.

I saw myself dying with a desire to see God, and I knew not how to seek that life other than by dying. Over my spirit flash and float in divine radiancy the bright and glorious visions of the world to which I go.

— SAINT TERESA OF AVILA

I solemnly assure you, the man who hears my word and has faith in Him who sent me possesses eternal life. An hour is coming, has indeed come, when the dead shall hear the voice of the Son of God, and those who have heeded it shall live.

— JESUS, JOHN 5:24-25 NAB

On the Missionaries of Charity

*What is required of a Missionary of Charity is this:
health of mind and body, ability to learn, a good dose
of good sense, and a joyous character.*

— MOTHER TERESA

*There is one more thing you must do. Go and sell
what you have and give to the poor. . . . After that
come follow me.*

— JESUS, MARK 10:21 NAB

Our sisters and our brothers are called Missionaries of Charity. They are young people who are called to be the carriers of God's love. A missionary is one sent with a mission — a message to deliver. Just as Jesus was sent by His Father, we too are sent by Him and filled with His Spirit to be witnesses of His gospel of love and compassion, first in our communities and then in our apostolate among the poorest of the poor all over the world.

I knew that God wanted something from me. I was only twelve years old, living with my parents in Skopje, Yugoslavia (now Macedonia), when I first sensed the desire to become a nun. At that time there were some very good priests who helped boys and girls follow their vocation, according to God's call. It was then that I realized that my call was to the poor.

Between twelve and eighteen years of age I lost the desire to become a nun. But at eighteen years of age I decided to leave my home and enter the Sisters of Our Lady of Loreto. Since then I have never had the least doubt that I was right. It was God's will: He made the choice. The Sisters of Loreto were devoted to teaching, which is a genuine apostolate for Christ. But my specific vocation, within the religious vocation, was for the poorest poor. It was a call from inside my vocation — like a second vocation. It was a command to resign from Loreto, where I was happy, in order to serve the poor in the streets.

In 1946, when I was going by train to Darjeeling for some spiritual exercises, I sensed a call to renounce everything in order to follow Christ in the poor suburbs, to serve among the poorest poor.

❧

Our spiritual life is a life of reliance on God. Our work is our prayer because we carry it out through Jesus, in Jesus, and for the sake of Jesus.

A vocation is a gift of Christ. He has said, "I have chosen you." Every vocation must really belong to Christ. The work that we are called to accomplish is just a means to give concrete substance to our love for God.

Our vocation is nothing else but to belong to Christ. The work that we do is only a means to put our love for Christ into living action.

All the religious congregations — nuns, priests, even the Holy Father — all have the same vocation: to belong to Jesus. "I have chosen you to be mine." That's our vocation. Our means, how we spend our time, may be different. Our love for Jesus in action is only the means, just like clothes. I wear this, you wear that: It's a means. But a vocation is not a means. Vocation, for a Christian, is Jesus.

We all have been called by God. As missionaries we must be carriers of God's love, ready to go in haste, like Mary, in search of souls; burning lights that give light to all men; the salt of the earth; souls consumed with one desire: Jesus.

We must know exactly when we say *yes* to God what is in that *yes*. *Yes* means "I surrender," totally, fully, without any counting the cost, without any examination: "Is it all right? Is it convenient?" Our *yes* to God is without any reservations.

We will allow only God to make plans for the future, for yesterday has gone, tomorrow has not yet come, and we have only today to make Him known, loved, and served.

Total surrender to God must come in small details as it comes in big details. It's nothing but a single word: *Yes!* "I accept whatever you give, and I give whatever you take." It doesn't mean doing extraordinary things, understanding big things — it is a simple acceptance, because I have given myself to God, because I belong to Him.

If something belongs to me, I've got full power to use it as I want. I belong to Jesus — He can do to me whatever He wants.

Total surrender involves loving trust. You cannot surrender totally unless you trust lovingly and totally. Jesus trusted His Father because He knew Him, He knew of His love.

"My Father and I are one."

"The Father is in me and I am in the Father."

"I am not alone, the Father is with me."

"Father, into your hands I commend my Spirit."

Read Saint John's Gospel and see how many times Jesus used the word "Father."

We must be empty if we want God to fill us. We must be able to give ourselves so completely to God that He must be able to possess us. We must "Give whatever He takes and take whatever He gives."

Total abandonment consists of giving oneself fully to God because God has given Himself to us. If God, who owes us nothing, is willing to give us nothing less than Himself, can we respond by giving Him only a part of ourselves?

Renouncing myself, I give myself to God that He might live in me. How poor we would be if God had not given us the power to give ourselves over to Him! Instead, how rich we are right now! How easy it is to conquer God! We give ourselves to Him, and God becomes ours, and now we have nothing but God.

Persuaded of our nothingness and with the blessing of obedience we attempt all things, doubting nothing, for with God all things are possible.

We often say to Christ, "Make us partakers of Your suffering." But, when someone is insensitive to us, how easily we forget that this is the moment to share with Christ! It would be enough for us to remember that it is Jesus who gives us, through such a person or circumstance, the opportunity to do something beautiful for Him.

If there has been resentment in our hearts or if we have not accepted humiliation, we will not learn humility. We cannot learn humility from books. Jesus accepted humiliation. Jesus came to do the will of His Father, and He did it from the very beginning to the very end.

We must keep His interests continually in our hearts and minds, carrying our Lord to places where He has not walked before, fearless in doing the things He did, courageously going through danger and death with Him and for Him; ready to accept joyously the need to die daily if we want to bring souls to God, to pay the price He paid for souls — ever ready to go to any part of the world and to respect and appreciate unfamiliar customs of other peoples, their living conditions and language, willing to adapt ourselves if and when necessary, happy to undertake any labor and toil, and glad to make any sacrifice involved in our missionary life.

This imposes a great responsibility on us to fight against our own ego and love of comfort that would lead us to choose a comfortable and insignificant mediocrity. We are called upon to make our lives a rivalry with Christ; we are called upon to be warriors in saris, for the church needs fighters today. Our war cry has to be "Fight not flight."

The church of God needs saints today. We shall go freely in the name of Jesus, to towns and villages all over the world, even amid squalid and dangerous surroundings, with Mary the Immaculate Mother of Jesus, seeking out the spiritually poorest of the poor with God's own tender affection and proclaiming to them the Good News of salvation and hope, singing with them His songs, bringing to them His love, peace, and joy. In spirit, to every part of the vast creation of God, from the furthest planet to the depths of the sea, from one abandoned convent chapel to another abandoned church, from an abortion clinic in one city to a prison cell in another, from the source of a river in one continent to a lonely mountain cave in another, and even into heaven and the gates of hell, praying with and for each of God's creation to save and sanctify each one for whom the blood of the Son of God has been shed.

In the world today there are those whose struggle is for justice and human rights. We have no time for this because we are in daily and continuous contact with people who are starving for a piece of bread and for some affection.

Should I devote myself to the struggle for justice when the most needy people would die right in front of me for lack of a glass of milk?

Nevertheless, I want to state clearly that I do not condemn those who struggle for justice. I believe there are different options for the people of God. To me, the most important thing is to serve the neediest of people. By following the vocation of a Missionary of Charity, we stand before the world as ambassadors of peace by preaching the message of love in action that crosses all barriers of nationality, creed, or country.

In the slums the sisters should find a place where they will gather little street children, whoever they may be. Their very first concern is to make them clean, feed them and only then teach them, and prepare them for admission into regular schools. The love of God must be proposed to them in a simple, interesting, and attractive way.

If one of the sisters is not in at least a serene mood, I do not allow her to go visit the poor. The poor already have so many reasons to feel sad; how could we take them the affliction of our own personal bad moods?

There is so much unhappiness, so much misery everywhere. Our human nature stays with us from beginning to end. We must work hard every day to conquer ourselves.

We must ask for the grace to love one another. As Jesus said, "Love one another as I have loved you" (John 15:12 NAB). To be capable of doing that, our sisters live a life of prayer and sacrifice.

That is why we start our day with Communion and meditation.

Every evening when we return from our work, we gather in the chapel for an unbroken hour of adoration. In the stillness of dusk, we find peace in Christ's presence. This hour of intimacy with Jesus is something very beautiful. I have seen a great change in our congregation from the day we started having adoration every day. Our love for Jesus is more intimate. Our love for each other is more understanding. Our love for the poor is more compassionate.

Our sisters and brothers work for the poorest of the poor — the sick, the dying, the lepers, the abandoned children. But I can tell you that in all these years I have never heard the poor grumble or curse, nor have I seen any of them dejected with sadness. The poor are great people; they can accept very difficult things.

The indifference of people who walk by without picking up those whom we pick up is a confirmation of their ignorance and lack of faith. If they were convinced that the one who is lying on the ground is their brother or their sister, I think they would undoubtedly do something. Unfortunately, they do not know what compassion is, and they do not know those beings. If they understood them, they would immediately become aware of the greatness of those human beings who are lying on the sidewalks. They would love them naturally, and loving them would lead them to serve them.

To the world, it seems foolish that we delight in poor food, that we relish rough and insipid bulgur (wheat); possess only three sets of habits made of coarse cloth or old soutanes (cassocks), mend and patch them, take great care of them and refuse to have extra; enjoy walking in any shape and color of shoes; bathe with just a bucket of water in small bathing rooms; sweat and perspire but refuse to have a fan; go hungry and thirsty but refuse to eat in the houses of the people; refuse to have radios or gramophones, which could be relaxing to the racked nerves after the whole day's hard toil; walk distances in the rain and hot summer sun, or go cycling, travel by second-class tram, or third-class overcrowded trains; sleep on hard beds, giving up soft and thick mattresses, which would be soothing to the aching bodies after the whole day's hard work; kneel on the rough and thin carpets in the chapel, giving up soft and thick ones; delight in lying in the common wards in the hospital among the poor of Christ, when we could easily have private cabins; work like coolies at home and outside when we could easily employ servants and do only the light jobs; relish cleaning the toilets and dirt as though that was the most beautiful job in the world and call it all a tribute to God. To some we are wasting our precious life and burying our talents.

Yes, our lives are utterly wasted if we use only the light of reason. Our life has no meaning unless we look at Christ in His poverty.

Our beautiful work with and for the poor is a privilege and a gift for us. I think that if we go to the poor with that love, with only the desire to give God to them, to bring the joy of Christ (which is our strength) into their homes, if they look at us and see Jesus and His love and compassion in us, I think the world will soon be full of peace and love.

Truly, the tenderness of God's love is most

extraordinary. When we look at the cross, we know how much Jesus loved us then. When we look at the tabernacle, we know how much He loves us now. Be alone with Jesus. Then your hearts will feel the joy that only He can give.

Try to put worship into practice in your life. You will notice a change in your life, in your family, in your parish, and in your environment. The Church is each one of us — you and I.

"I have called you by your name," Jesus said. "You are mine. You are precious in my sight. I love you." If you love Christ, it will be easy for you to fully belong to Jesus and to give Jesus to everyone you find.

God loves me. I'm not here just to fill a place, just to be a number. He has chosen me for a purpose. I know it.

Dear Lord:

Help me to spread your fragrance wherever I go.

Flood my soul with your spirit and life.

Penetrate and possess my whole being so utterly that all my life may only be a radiance of yours.

Shine through me, and be so in me that every soul I come in contact with may feel your presence in my soul.

Let them look up and see no longer me, but only you, O Lord!

Stay with me, then I shall begin to shine as you do; so to shine as to be a light to others.

The light, O Lord, will be all from you; none of it will be mine; it will be you shining on others through me.

Let me thus praise you in the way you love best, by shining on those around me.

Let me preach you without preaching, not by words but by my example, by the catching force, the sympathetic influence of what I do, the evident fullness of the love my heart bears to you.

Amen.

— JOHN HENRY NEWMAN
(ONE OF MOTHER TERESA'S FAVORITE PRAYERS,
SAID EVERY DAY BY THE MISSIONARIES OF CHARITY.)

I am the light of the world. Whoever follows me will never walk in darkness but will have the light of life.

— JESUS, JOHN 8:12 RSV

Mother Teresa:
A Conversation

Love has a hem to her garment
That reaches the very dust.
It sweeps the stains
From the streets and lanes,
And because it can, it must.

— MOTHER TERESA

Come, O blessed of my Father,
inherit the kingdom prepared for you
from the foundation of the world;
for I was hungry and you gave me food,
I was thirsty and you gave me drink,
I was a stranger and you welcomed me,
I was naked and you clothed me,
I was sick and you visited me,
I was in prison and you came to me. . . .
As you did it to one of the least of these my brethren,
you did it to me.

— JESUS, MATTHEW 25:34-36, 40, RSV

In this interview Mother Teresa talks candidly about the order she founded, about her world-wide work with "the poorest of the poor," and about her faith. It is based on several conversations between Mother Teresa and Jose Luis Bonzales-Balado.

Mother Teresa, do you find it easy to carry out your work among the poor?

Of course it would not be easy without an intense life of prayer and a spirit of sacrifice. It wouldn't be easy either if we didn't see the poor — Christ — who continue to suffer the sorrows of

His passion. At times, we would be happy if we could get the poor to live peacefully with each other. It is so hard for those who have been deprived of their basic needs to live in harmony and support their neighbors, and not see them as dangerous competitors, capable of making their state of misery even worse! That's why we cannot offer them anything but our testimony of love, seeing Christ Himself in each one of them, no matter how repugnant they seem to us.

How do you get so many vocations?

God is the one who sends them. They come and see. Sometimes they come from very far away. Many of them first hear about us by what they read in the newspapers.

With the sisters you have available, do you accomplish all that you would like?

Unfortunately, the needs are always greater than our ability to meet them.

Mother Teresa, what moves you to continually open new homes?

If God continues sending us so many vocations without fail, we believe that this is not so we can keep them hidden in convents. Rather, God wants to multiply the work of helping the poorest of the poor.

What criteria do you use for opening homes in India and abroad?

We never open any home without already having been invited by the local bishop. In fact, the present requests for help far surpass our capability to meet them. As a general rule based on our Constitution, when we receive an invitation to open a new home, we first go and investigate the living conditions of the poor in that area. We never decide to open a home for any other reason than that of serving the poor. Normally, the decision to start a new home follows these investigations, except in cases of the most extreme need.

What importance do you give to outward appearances?

Very little or none. As for our habit, even though the sari is part of our usual way of dressing, we would be willing to modify or relinquish it if we found out that we were not accepted for being dressed that way. We would adopt another form of dress if it were better accepted by the poor wherever we felt called to carry out our work.

What gives you strength to carry out your work?

We are taught from the very first moment to discover Christ under the distressing disguise of the poor, the sick, the outcasts. Christ presents Himself to us under every disguise: the dying, the paralytic, the leper, the invalid, the orphan. It is faith that makes our work, which demands both special preparation and a special calling, easy or at least more bearable. Without faith, our work could become an obstacle for our religious life since we come across blasphemy, wickedness, and atheism at every turn.

*In your work, how much importance do you give
to religious matters?*

We are not simply social workers, but missionaries. Nevertheless, we try to do evangelization exclusively through our work, allowing God to manifest Himself in it. We teach catechism to the children in our orphanages. We only take the initiative with adults when they ask for instruction or when they ask us questions about religious matters. All of the sisters receive a good religious formation during their novitiate and more training in later years. We do not like to take the place of others who are more competent in some subjects than we are. For example, we refer more difficult questions to priests, besides those that are obviously related to their ministry. As for the criteria we use to determine our assistance, we never base our assistance on the religious beliefs of the needy but on the need itself. We are not concerned with the religious beliefs of those we help. We only focus on how urgent the need is.

Do the Missionaries of Charity have any preferences among the people they assist?

If there is any, it is for the poorest of the poor, the most abandoned, those who have no one to care for them, the orphans, the dying, the lepers.

According to some, the work of the Missionaries of Charity in the home for the dying destitutes only prolongs the misery of those cared for. Those who are restored to health return to the streets where they will encounter the same problems of disease and misery. What is your response to this?

Whenever it is possible we try not to limit our care to just medical attention. We try to achieve the human and social rehabilitation of those who are restored to health. It is true that in many cases those who recuperate prefer the freedom of the streets to the closed spaces of our surroundings, but this is something that we cannot prevent. We act under the conviction that every time we feed the poor, we are offering food to Christ Himself. Whenever we clothe a naked human being, we are clothing Christ

Himself. Whenever we offer shelter to the dying, we are sheltering Christ Himself.

> *There are those who assert that the medical train-ing of the Missionaries of Charity is too rudi-mentary for people who care for the seriously ill.*

I know that. Our medical training is limited, but we try to offer assistance and care to those who, in most cases, have no one to give them even the most basic medical care.

> *It has also been said that the care that you give to such desperate cases could be better channeled to those who have a better chance of survival.*

We try to help all those who need care, but we give preference to those who have the greatest need of help. We do not turn our backs on anyone.

No one is left out of our will to serve. In each suffering brother we see the likeness of Christ suffering in him. Even if we have to narrow our care down to a few, because of necessity or limited resources, our desire is to expand our charity.

At times, there isn't much you do or can do for
the dying, is there?

We can, at least, leave them with the impression
of something important: that there are people willing to truly love them, because the dying are also
children of God, and deserve to be loved as much or
maybe even more than anyone else.

Don't you ever experience repugnance in the face
of so much misery?

Yes, we carry out our work mainly among the
dying, the destitute elderly, poor, orphaned children, and lepers. We cannot deny that our work is
hard for us in many cases. We don't always carry it
out under acceptable conditions. But all of us are
better off working among the poor than among the
rich. This is our lifetime work. During the novitiate,
which lasts two years, we dedicate half the day to
carrying out our work among the poor. The novices
work under the supervision of older sisters. Then,
before making our final vows, we spend several
more years serving the poor. Our work becomes

almost a habit for us, which makes it easier, instinctive, and natural, without being mechanical.

> *What significance do you attribute to your*
> *mission of assistance?*

Our service is not limited to offering just material relief. We want to offer whatever is necessary so that the poorest of the poor don't feel abandoned, and so they realize that there are people who care about them. We want our work to accomplish what a high-level official in our country once said to the sisters: "It is Christ who is again walking among us doing good in favor of men."

> *What do you do for lepers?*

We offer assistance to more than twenty thousand afflicted with this disease just in Calcutta alone, and to fifty thousand in all of India. We realize this is nothing in a country where there are four million victims of leprosy. The first thing we do for those who receive our help is to convince them that they really have this disease. We get the necessary medicines for them and we try to cure them. Today it is not necessary for lepers to live in isolation. If we can help them in time, they can be fully cured. So what the sisters try to do first of all is to convince the people to confront this disease. In India, leprosy is considered a punishment from God. It is part of the religion of the people. The sisters try to do everything possible to cure them and rid them of this belief.

From whom do you especially receive aid?

From everyone, thanks be to God. We have Hindu, Muslim, Parsee, Jewish, Buddhist, Protestant, and, naturally, Catholic Co-workers and benefactors.

Has it ever occurred to you that you could end up without resources for your works?

We never have any surplus, but we have never lacked what we need. Sometimes it happens in strange ways, almost miraculously. We wake up without resources, with the anguish of not being able to tend to our needy. A few hours later, we almost always see the most unexpected provisions arrive from anonymous donors. From Catholics, Protestants, Buddhists, Jews, Parsees, Muslims, and Hindus. From adherents of any religion or of no religion. From the rich and from the poor.

What is the work you accomplish like?

It is not important work in and of itself, but the humblest that exists. We think that its value comes from the spirit of love for God that inspires it. It is impossible to love God without loving our neighbor. At the same time, no Missionary of Charity forgets the words of Christ: "I was hungry and you gave me to eat" (see Matthew 25:35). This is what we are trying to do: feed, clothe, and visit Christ in the sick, the dying, the lepers, and the abandoned children.

Could you talk about your work with abandoned children?

Yes, we started with them and we are still with

them, even though they are not our only work. Orphans and abandoned children are unfortunately the kind of children that are never in short supply. Once in the first years of our work, a policeman brought us a group of children that were caught in the act of stealing. They were too young to send to jail with common criminals. I asked them why they had done it. They explained to me that every evening from five to eight o'clock adults gave them lessons on how to commit robberies.

What kind of a future do the children you rescue have?

I don't believe there is a better way of helping India than to prepare a better tomorrow for today's children. We take care of the poorest of those children, the ones that are picked up in the slums. Each one of them needs a monthly allowance of just a few dollars. It is very moving to see children from other countries — French, English, German, Spanish, Swiss, Danish, and Italian children — donate from their savings. We open a savings account for each child we take in. When the child is older and if he is capable, he receives higher education. We see that those children who do not have the aptitude for higher education receive an education in the trades, so that they will be able to make a living for themselves.

You Missionaries of Charity witness terrible injustices. How do you react to them?

The injustices are there for everyone to see. It is up to large organizations to provide or promote the ways of raising the standard of living of the masses that suffer injustice. We find ourselves in daily contact with those who have been rejected by society. Our first goal is to help these people achieve basic human development. We try to restore the sense of dignity that they should have as human beings, as well as children of the same Father. To accomplish this, we don't look first and see if they are dying or if they have a whole life ahead of them.

Do you receive any aid from the Indian government?

We do not receive any direct aid, but we have to recognize that the government helps us in a very effective way by the confidence, esteem, and respect they show us. This helps us in many ways, like getting land for the work we carry out and free transportation on the state railways.

Do you receive any exemptions from the Indian government? Are you allowed to import everything freely?

No, not everything, just food, medicines, medical equipment, clothing, and anything else that is needed for our work, such as furniture, typewriters, and sewing machines. We still need an import permit. We receive these things as gifts, and they all go to the poor. Nothing is for business transactions. It all goes to those in need, without regard to their race, beliefs, or religion. And there are so many in need! The only thing we have to do is declare to the government that these are free gifts. Since the government sees where everything goes, we are given the necessary permits. They realize that nothing goes into our pockets. Everything is given back to the poorest of the poor. That's why they trust us and give us the necessary permits.

How do you manage what you receive?

We have a register where we write down all our expenses, as well as what we receive and for what purpose we have to earmark those gifts. For example, if someone donates one hundred rupees for the lepers, we don't use that money for anything else. We try to carry out the will of our donors.

It seems that the Indian government is setting increasingly tighter restrictions on foreign missionaries. Are you affected by this?

We are a native Indian institution. Our mother-house is in India. So we don't fall under those restrictions. At the same time, we avoid evangelizing through means other than our work. Our works are our witness. If someone we help wants to become a

Catholic, he has to see a priest. If there is a religious end to our work, it is nothing more than to bring all those we have contact with closer to God.

Do you receive any help from others?

Oh, yes! We have counted on the help of others since the very beginning. We call them Co-workers. We have many kinds of Co-workers, starting with the children from many countries who share their savings or the money they collect on drives for the children in India. Even though we Missionaries have the most visibility, really, we would carry out very little of our work without the generous help of thousands upon thousands of Co-workers and friends throughout the world.

Not all religious orders have known how to faithfully keep the initial spirit in which they were founded. Couldn't the Missionaries of Charity lose it also?

Our fourth vow commits us to give free service to the poorest of the poor. This should keep us from the danger you mention. Our mission is so clear that there can be no misunderstandings. The poor know who they are and where they are. They are the reason for our order and our work. In Christ, they are the reason why we exist.

> *Are you ever tempted with the idea of working among the rich, where everything would be easier for you?*

The poor are the reason for our existence. We were born for them and we dedicate ourselves just to them, without any temptation to turn away.

> *Do you attempt to present any special religious message through your work?*

Love has no other message but its own. Every day we try to live out Christ's love in a very tangible way, in every one of our deeds. If we do any preaching, it is done with deeds, not with words. That is our witness to the gospel.

❦

Do you feel loved by the people?

Yes, for the most part, even though the extreme conditions in which many of our people live keeps them from seeing our unconditional love. They see that we live among them and in poverty like they do. They appreciate that a lot. Still, not everything is peaceful all the time. Sometimes there are outbreaks of jealousy or impatience when we can't give them everything they need or ask for, or when they see that we are giving out the very things they want to others more needy than themselves. When that happens, we know it is useless to try to reason with them at that moment. It is best to allow them to calm down. They almost always have a change of attitude once they have calmed down.

Do you witness conversions to Catholicism among the people you help?

Yes, there are some conversions, but without us ever trying to encourage them directly. By practicing Christian love, we draw closer to God and we try to help others draw closer to Him, without placing any religious pressure on anyone. When they accept love, they accept God and vice versa. Our witness is none other than that. At the same time, it would be a mistake to forget that we find ourselves in India, among a people proud of their cultural and religious traditions. For that very reason they look with distrust upon any form of religious proselytism.

What contact do the Missionaries of Charity have with their families?

Once we are consecrated to serving the poor, they become our family. Naturally, we do not deny our blood relationships with our biological families, but contact with them is very limited. Only under extraordinary circumstances, such as before leaving the country for a foreign mission, do we go home. We just cannot do it, first of all because of our poverty; we do not have the money to spend on trips. Second, none of us can leave our post of service and care to the sick, the dying, the lepers, and the orphans when they have no one else to look after them.

What do you think of receiving awards?

The same as always: I don't deserve them. I accept them willingly, not just to acknowledge the kindness of those who give the awards, but I think of what these awards can mean for our poor and our lepers. I think that these awards greatly help people to be favorably inclined toward the work we Missionaries of Charity carry out among the poorest of the poor.

O JESUS

— *You who suffer, grant that, today and every day, I may be able to see you in the person of your sick ones and that, by offering them my care, I may serve you.*

Grant that, even if you are hidden under the unattractive disguise of anger, of crime, or of madness, I may recognize you and say, "Jesus, you who suffer, how sweet it is to serve you."

Give me, Lord, this vision of faith, and my work will never be monotonous, I will find joy in harboring the small whims and desires of all the poor who suffer.

Dear sick one, you are still more beloved to me because you represent Christ. What a privilege I am granted in being able to take care of you!

O God, since you are Jesus who suffers, deign to be for me also a Jesus who is patient, indulgent with my faults, who looks only at my intentions, which are to love you and to serve you in the person of each of these children of yours who suffer.

Lord, increase my faith. Bless my efforts and my work, now and forever.

— MOTHER TERESA

SOMETHING BEAUTIFUL FOR GOD

Come with me into a world of poverty,
Into a land where men are dying endlessly,
Into a world of inhumanity.
Can't you see they're starving, where's your charity?
They laugh and cry, they're people just like you and me,
They need help and not just sympathy.

CHORUS:

Show each one something beautiful for God above,
 Something beautiful to show your love,
 Something beautiful for God above,
 Something beautiful to show your love.

 A day goes by, the night is long for everyone.
 A child is crying, perhaps he'll live to see the sun,
 And yet he knows the morning may not come.
 Throughout the world our brothers live in
poverty,
 They're everywhere, if only we have eyes to see,
 So look around and find your sanity.
 Show to men the love that He has shown to you,

And feed His lambs as He has fed each one of you,
He loves them as much as He loves you.

— MOTHER TERESA

Mother Teresa:
A Biographical Sketch

. . . Behold thy Mother!

— JESUS, JOHN 19:26 KJV

Born in southeastern Europe in 1910, Agnes Gonxha Bojaxhiu (Mother Teresa) became a nun among the destitute masses of the Calcutta slums. In time, her work grew to span the globe, causing her to become one of the best known and most highly respected women in the world. Winner of many awards, including the Nobel Peace Prize and the Templeton Award for Progress in Religion, she is personally acquainted with popes, presidents, and royalty. She has never hesitated, however, to do the most menial tasks, and one of her oft-repeated themes is the need for humility. Today there are over four thousand religious sisters and brothers internationally in the 107 houses founded by the Missionaries of Charity.

The psalmist's description of God's loyal

followers fits Mother Teresa: "They that are plant-
ed in the house of the Lord shall flourish in the
courts of our God. They shall bear fruit even in old
age; vigorous and sturdy shall they be, Declaring
how just is the Lord, my Rock, in whom there is no
wrong" (PSALM 92:14-16 NAB).

August 16, 1910: A daughter is born to the
Bojaxhiu family. The child who will one day be
known as Mother Teresa is born in Skopje, capital
of the Albanian republic of Macedonia. She is the
third and last child of Nikolle Bojaxhiu and Drana
Bernai, married in 1900. Her sister, Aga, was born
in 1905 and her brother, Lazar, was born in 1907.

August 27, 1910: The child is baptized in the
parish church of the Sacred Heart of Jesus and
given the name Gonxha (Agnes). Her parents are
devout Catholics, especially her mother.

1919: Nikolle Bojaxhiu dies of an apparent
poisoning after attending a political meeting. He

was a municipal councilman with strong nationalist convictions.

1915-24: Agnes has a happy childhood. Along with her brother and her sister, Agnes attends public school. She does well, even though her health is somewhat delicate. She also attends catechism classes at the parish, joins the parish choir, and belongs to a Catholic youth organization called the Daughters of Mary. She has special interest in reading about missionaries and the lives of the saints.

Mother Teresa sums up her family life during her childhood and adolescence: "We were all very united, especially after the death of my father. We lived for each other and we made every effort to make one another happy. We were a very united and a very happy family."

Lazar, the only son, commented about the religious life of his mother and sisters: "We lived next to the parish church of the Sacred Heart of Jesus. Sometimes my mother and sisters seemed to live as much in the church as they did at home. They were always involved with the choir, the religious services, and missionary topics."

Lazar also commented about his mother's generosity: "She never allowed any of the many poor people who came to our door to leave empty-handed. When we would look at her strangely, she would say, 'Keep in mind that even those who are not our blood relatives, even if they are poor, are still our brethren.'"

At the age of twelve, Agnes feels her first gentle calling to the religious and missionary life, a calling that will lie dormant for several years. Meanwhile, she continues being an active member of the Daughters of Mary. With the encouragement of her parish priests, who are Jesuits, she grows in her interest in missionary outreach. Agnes' brother, Lazar, moves to Austria to study at a military academy to become a cavalry officer.

1928: Agnes' interest in missionary outreach is

confirmed by a clear calling to the religious life
while she is praying before the altar of the Patroness
of Skopje: "Our Lady interceded for me and helped
me to discover my vocation." With the guidance
and help of a Yugoslav Jesuit, Agnes applies for
admission to the Order of the Sisters of Our Lady
of Loreto (commonly called the Irish Ladies),
founded in the sixteenth century by Mary Ward.
She is attracted by their missionary work in India.

September 26, 1928: Admitted provisionally,
Agnes sets out on her trip to Dublin, traveling by
train through Yugoslavia, Austria, Switzerland,
France, and England until she arrives at the mother-
house of the Sisters of Our Lady of Loreto.

December 1, 1928: After two months of inten-
sive English language studies, Agnes sets out by ship
for India, arriving on January 6, 1929, after thirty-
seven days. Agnes stays in Calcutta only one week,
after which she is sent to Darjeeling, in the foothills
of the Himalayas, to begin her novitiate.

May 24, 1931: After two years as a novice,

Agnes professes temporary vows as a Sister of Our Lady of Loreto, changing her baptismal name to Teresa. "I chose the name Teresa for my religious vows. But it wasn't the name of the great Teresa of Avila. I chose the name of Teresa of the Little Flower, Therese of Lisieux."

1931-37: After professing her temporary vows, Sister Teresa lives in Calcutta and serves as a geography and history teacher at St. Mary's School, run by the Sisters of Our Lady of Loreto.

May 24, 1937: After renewing her temporary vows several times, Sister Teresa professes her final vows as a Sister of Our Lady of Loreto, eventually becoming the director of studies at St. Mary's. Mother Teresa sums up her life in the religious order: "I was the happiest nun at Loreto. I dedicated myself to teaching. That job, carried out for the love of God, was a true apostolate. I liked it very much."

September 10, 1946: God calls her to serve the poor. Mother Teresa calls it "a day of inspiration." She says, "While I was going by train from Calcutta to Darjeeling to participate in spiritual exercises, I was quietly praying when I clearly felt a call within my calling. The message was very clear. I had to leave the convent and consecrate myself to helping the poor by living among them. It was a command I knew where I had to go, but I did not know how to get there."

1948: Leaving the Sisters of Our Lady of Loreto is difficult and painful for Sister Teresa. To do so, she needs special permission from Rome after an agreement is reached within her religious order. Finally, the permission is granted for her to live as a nun outside of the convent. She leaves on August 16, after taking off the religious habit of the Sisters of Our Lady of Loreto and putting on a white sari that looks like the ones worn by the poorest women in India. The sari has a blue border symbolizing her desire to imitate the Virgin Mary. Mother Teresa leaves Calcutta to take an accelerated three-month course in basic nursing, then returns to put into practice her desire to dedicate herself to serving the poorest of the poor in the slums of Calcutta. This year she also applies for and is granted lifelong Indian citizenship.

March 19, 1949: The first follower joins Mother Teresa. Subashini Das, an old student of Mother Teresa, visits her unexpectedly and says that she wants to join her. She will be the first nun of a religious order yet to exist.

July 10, 1950: The Order of Missionaries of Charity is authorized by Rome. Other young women follow Subashini Das at a promising rate. Mother Teresa says, "After 1949, I saw young women arriving one after another. All of them had been students of mine. They wanted to give everything to God and they were in a hurry to do so."

October 7, 1950: The feast of Our Lady of the Rosary, Rome authorizes the Order of the Missionaries of Charity. Ten women begin their novitiate, which lasts two years.

1952: The home for dying destitutes is opened. There are nearly thirty women in the order. A dozen of them have made their final vows. There are twelve novices and the rest are postulants. The sisters are still in need of a convent of their own. They are "guests" in a rented flat, donated to them by Michael Gomes. They dedicate themselves to studies and religious formation, while caring for abandoned slum children and sick and dying destitutes. Mother Teresa manages to acquire a home for the destitutes in Kalighat, a Hindu temple in the heart of Calcutta. The home is opened on August 22, the feast of Mary Immaculate, and is immediately filled to capacity, which will always be the case through the years in spite of the constant "discharges" (there are always new admittances). The home is named Nirmal Hriday, "Home of the Pure Heart," a name that is just as acceptable to Hindus, who are a great majority of those coming to the home.

1953: The motherhouse of the Missionaries of Charity is founded. After "storming" heaven with constant prayers, the Missionaries of Charity are able to buy a home for their convent, located at 54 Lower Circular Road in Calcutta. The home is well located for their needs and temporarily spacious.

The motherhouse will become the central head-quarters for the Missionaries of Charity. On the same street, the sisters rent and later buy a home for abandoned and orphaned slum children. Many of the parents of these children have died in the home for dying destitutes. The sisters initially want to open a home also for the lepers they care for. However, due to the opposition of the general population, they start up "mobile clinics" for lepers. Later the sisters will be able to open self-sufficient rehabilitation centers for lepers, called Titagahr and Shanti Nagar, on the outskirts of Calcutta.

1962: Mother Teresa is honored with the Padna Sri (Order of the Lotus) Award given to her by the Indian government, and the Magsaysay Award given to her by the SEATO nations of southeastern Asia. Despite her recognition in Asia, she is still largely unknown in the West.

February 1, 1965: The Missionaries of Charity receive further recognition. They have now existed for fifteen years and have had extraordinary growth and expansion. There are approximately three hundred sisters in the order — including sisters of different European nationalities — and several homes. All of the Missionaries of Charity homes are still located in India under the jurisdiction of the local Catholic bishops. With the support of several bishops, Pope Paul VI decrees the praise-worthiness of the Missionaries of Charity, giving "validity" to the order for the wider Catholic Church. This decree, along with an invitation from the Archbishop of Barquisimeto, Venezuela, to open a home in his diocese, enables the Missionaries of Charity to expand their missionary work.

1965-71: New homes are opened around the world. The home in Venezuela is Mother Teresa's first home "abroad." During the following years, more homes are opened in Africa, in Australia (Melbourne and Adelaide), and in Europe (England and Italy), as a response to invitations extended by local Catholic bishops. The Missionaries of Charity's first home in Rome, Italy, is founded in response to an invitation extended by Pope Paul VI, as Bishop of Rome. The Pope is an admirer and benefactor of Mother Teresa's work and grants her

Vatican citizenship to facilitate her missionary travels. In 1971 the Missionaries of Charity have fifty homes.

March 3, 1969: Pope Paul VI approves the statutes for the Co-workers and thereby they become officially affiliated with the Missionaries of Charity.

March 26, 1969: The Co-workers of the Missionaries of Charity are officially established. Mother Teresa's Co-workers, an international organization of lay men and women, become a spiritual reality and an important element for furthering the work of the Missionaries of Charity. It is difficult, if not impossible, to ascertain their number due to their constant growth. There have been Co-workers ever since the Missionaries of Charity were first founded.

1970s: Mother Teresa receives major international awards. The pen and microphone of Malcolm Muggeridge, a British journalist, makes Mother Teresa famous in the West, not only in

Catholic circles but in wider society. As a consequence, she is awarded the Good Samaritan Award in the United States, the Templeton Award for Progress in Religion in England, and the Pope John XXIII Peace Prize at the Vatican.

July 12, 1972: Mother Teresa's mother, Drana Bernai, dies in Albania. Her mother wanted to leave Albania in order to see her daughter as well as her son, who lives in Sicily, before she died. The Albanian government refused to grant her permission to leave.

1974: Mother Teresa's only sister, Aga Bojaxhiu, dies in Albania without having the opportunity to see either her sister or brother.

October 17, 1979: Mother Teresa is awarded the most famous international award: the Nobel Peace Prize. Nevertheless, her habitual simplicity and humility are not altered.

December 10, 1979: Mother Teresa accepts the Nobel Peace Prize from the hands of King Olaf V of Norway, in the name of the poor whom she represents and to whom she has dedicated her life.

1980-85: The Missionaries of Charity open many new homes and are blessed with many new vocations. In 1980 there are fourteen homes outside of India, in places as diverse as Lebanon, West Germany, Yugoslavia, Mexico, Brazil, Peru, Kenya, Haiti, Spain, Ethiopia, Belgium, New Guinea, and Argentina. After the Nobel Peace Prize is awarded, the Missionaries of Charity's rate of expansion is surprising: Eighteen new homes are opened in 1981, twelve in 1982, and fourteen in 1983. The Missionaries of Charity are also blessed with an increasing rate of new vocations, making the order an exception in an era of general decline in the number of new vocations for religious orders.

1986-89: The order enters countries previously closed to missionaries. The Missionaries of Charity are allowed to open homes in Ethiopia and Southern Yemen. Also they are allowed to come to Nicaragua, Cuba, and Russia, where atheism is actively promoted by the state. In the case of the

Soviet Union, one of the fruits of Mikhail Gorbachev's "perestroika" is permission for Mother Teresa to open a home in Moscow.

February 1986: Pope John Paul II comes to Calcutta. The Pope visits Mother Teresa and sees firsthand the work of the Missionaries of Charity.

May 21, 1988: The Missionaries of Charity open a shelter for the homeless in Rome at the Vatican. It is called "A Gift from Mary" to commemorate the Marian Year. The shelter has seventy-two beds for men and women and two dining halls, one for residents and one for those who stop in. The shelter also has a lounge, an infirmary, and a patio which faces the Pope Paul VI audience hall.

1988-89: Mother Teresa is hospitalized twice due to heart trouble. It is not the first time that she has overextended herself to the point of physical exhaustion and been hospitalized. Even the Pope asks her to take better care of her health. Her doctors install a pacemaker and order her to take six months of rest.

April 16, 1990: Citing ill health as the main reason, Mother Teresa steps down as the Superior General of her order. Relieved of her responsibilities, she is able to spend more time traveling and visiting various houses of sisters.

September 1990: Even though she is now eighty years old and in ill health, Mother Teresa is called out of retirement and reelected the Superior General of the Missionaries of Charity.

January 1991: Mother Teresa appeals to two heads of state to avert the Gulf War. Presidents George Bush and Saddam Hussein received her impassioned plea on behalf of "the innocent ones" only a short time before war erupted. Two teams of sisters go to Baghdad to minister to those ravaged by war.

1991-1993: Mother Teresa's health declines. Her failing heart causes Mother Teresa to collapse first in Tijuana, Mexico and again in Delhi, India. Despite her own suffering, she rallies when she is invited to return to Beijing in October 1993.

August 30, 1993: Her failing health prompts Mother Teresa to instruct that only those who work directly with the Missionaries of Charity can continue to be called Co-workers. All others no longer formally tied to the Missionaries of Charity are disbanded.

February 3, 1994: National Prayer Breakfast, Washington, D.C. Flanked by President and Mrs. Clinton and Vice President and Mrs. Gore, Mother Teresa speaks as thousands of people listen with rapt attention to her message affirming life and calling for peace. Later, the President thanks her for "her life of commitment," a commitment, he says, that she has "truly lived."

April 1996: After falling out of bed at the Missionaries of Charity headquarters, Mother Teresa is admitted briefly to the hospital with a broken collarbone.

August 1996: Mother Teresa is admitted to the hospital in Calcutta with malarial fever. The fever aggravates her long-standing heart condition and she develops a lung infection from prolonged use of a respirator. After several trips in and out of the hospital, she is allowed to return to her work.

October 1996: President Bill Clinton signs legislation making Mother Teresa an honorary U.S. citizen. In signing the bill, Clinton says, Mother Teresa has "brought hope and love into the lives of millions of orphaned and abandoned children the world over."

If you appreciated *No Greater Love,*
we highly recommend the following
from New World Library:

The Words of Christ

In *The Words of Christ,* editor Dale Salwak distills
the essence of Jesus' words from the four canonical
gospels, the Acts of the Apostles, I & II Corinthians,
and Revelation, and arranges them thematically.

By brilliantly presenting the heart of Christianity,
The Words of Christ serves as a powerful reminder of the
source of our traditions and of what is possible if we
read and heed these words.

If you would like to join us in supporting the work of Mother Teresa, contact the Missionaries of Charity nearest you, or write:

The Missionaries of Charity
1596 Fulton Street
San Francisco, CA 94117

New World Library is dedicated to publishing books and cassettes that inspire and challenge us to improve the quality of our lives and our world. For a catalog of our fine books and cassettes contact:

New World Library
14 Pamaron Way, Novato, CA 94949
Phone: (415) 884-2100
FAX: (415) 884-2199

Or call toll free: (800) 227-3900